THE FACE OF THE FATHER

An Exclusive Interview with Barbara Centilli
Concerning her Revelations and Visions of
God our Father

DEDICATION AND CONSECRATION

This book is dedicated to my good friend and father figure, Dr. Monroe Schneier, and to all of the Jewish people, to whom our Heavenly Father first revealed His face and to whom He promises to touch again in a special way. It is consecrated to the loving and paternal heart of the Eternal Father, whose boundless Love for all mankind is clearly visible in so many ways and in so many lives each and every day.

Copyright © 1999 St. Andrew's Productions
All Rights Reserved

ISBN: 1-891903-19-5

Published by:

St. Andrew's Productions
6111 Steubenville Pike
McKees Rocks, PA 15136

Tel: (412) 787-9735
Fax: (412) 787-5204

www.SaintAndrew.com

PRINTED IN THE UNITED STATES OF AMERICA

ACKNOWLEDGMENTS

I am indebted to many for assisting and supporting me with this work, especially Barbara Rose Centilli, Robert and Kim Petrisko, Dr. Frank Novasack, Fr. Richard Whetstone - JCOL, Michael Fontecchio, Amanda DeFazio, Carole McElwain, Carol Jean Speck, Joan Smith, Jim Petrilena, Clyde Gualandri, Sister Agnes McCormick, Janice T. Connell, Mary Lou Sokol, and the prayer group at the Pittsburgh Center for Peace.

My loving appreciation to my family; my wife Emily, daughters Maria, Sarah and Natasha, and son, Joshua.

ABOUT THE AUTHOR

Dr. Thomas W. Petrisko was the President of the Pittsburgh Center for Peace from 1990 to 1998 and he has served as editor of the Center's six "Queen of Peace" special edition newspapers. These papers were published in many millions throughout the world. He is the author of numerous articles and has written thirteen books on the subject of apparitions, miracles, and supernatural events occuring in the world today: *Call of the Ages, The Sorrow, the Sacrifice and the Triumph, For the Soul of the Family, Mother of the Secret, The Last Crusade, False Prophets of Today, The Prophecy of Daniel, St. Joseph and the Triumph of the Saints, In God's Hands: The Miraculous Story of Little Audrey Santo, The Fatima Prophecies: At the Doorstep of the World, The Kingdom of Our Father, Glory to the Father and The Face of the Father.*

Dr. Petrisko, along with his wife Emily, have three daughters, Maria, Sarah, Natasha, a son, Joshua, and a baby due in August of 1999.

The decree of the Congregation for the Propagation of the Faith (AAS 58, 1186 - approved by Pope Paul VI on 14 October 1966) ruled that the Nihil Obstat and Imprimatur are no longer required for publications that deal with private revelations, apparitions, prophecies, miracles, etc., provided nothing is said in contradiction of faith and morals.

The author hereby affirms his unconditional submission to whatever final judgment is delivered by the Church regarding the events currently under investigation in this book.

TABLE OF CONTENTS

FOREWORD 1
1 - I AM THE FATHER OF ALL MANKIND 5
2 - CONSECRATE YOURSELVES TO ME 11
3 - THE FEAST IS FOR MY CHILDREN 17
4 - IT IS I, YOUR FATHER AND YOUR GOD 23
5 - MY KINGDOM 29
6 - I FEEL ALL THAT MY CHILDREN FEEL 35
7 - CALLED BY THE FATHER 43
8 - IN THE PRESENCE OF THE FATHER 51
9 - THE FATHER REVEALS HIS PLAN 57
10 - CONSECRATION TO OUR FATHER 63
11 - THE LOVE OF THE FATHER 69
12 - HONORING OUR FATHER 73
13 - THE FATHER OF ALL MANKIND 79
14 - A PURIFICATION? 81
15 - THE COMING OF THE KINGDOM 85
16 - THE FEAST DAY, THE MEDAL, AND THE SCAPULAR 91
17 - FATIMA AND THE FATHER 95
18 - GETTING CLOSER TO OUR FATHER 101
19 - SEEING WITH THE EYES OF OUR SOUL 105
20 - SPREADING DEVOTION TO OUR FATHER 109

INTRODUCTION

I conducted the interview with Mrs. Centilli contained in this book over the latter half of 1998 and the early months of 1999. During this time, I was constantly impressed with her candid and profound understanding of the Father and His plan for all mankind. But most of all I was deeply moved by her great humility and lack of pretension, so much so that I gradually became of the opinion that truly the Father had chosen and prepared a unique and special soul to deliver His message through at this time in history.

While there have been many private revelations given over the centuries to illuminate our faith in God, many believe that the reported dialogue between Barbara Centilli and God the Father is a masterpiece of spirituality, something well beyond the norm. Contained in two published works, titled *Seeing With the Eyes of the Soul*, the Centilli revelations truly reveal the love, mercy, and understanding of Our Heavenly Father for His Children, His call for His children to consecrate themselves to Him, and His passionate desire for a Feast Day in His honor to celebrate their return home to His loving arms and warm embrace.

Now, Barbara Centilli has agreed to share even more with us about our Father, so much more that indeed, we can start to see the "Face of the Father." I pray that each soul who reads this account will do just that.

Thomas W. Petrisko
May 13, 1999

FOREWORD

You Shall See the Face of God
By Fr. Richard Whetstone, JCOL

All during his pontificate the Holy Father has been advising us not to be afraid in our approach to God. Man, as always, not listening to the words of a prophet, instead draws further and further away from this Loving God.

This loving Father, is continuously searching for ways in which to invite His creation back to what is theirs through His grace and concern for them.

We see how He left the heavens to search out Adam and Eve - His manifestation to Abraham - His visit to Moses. At all times His creation felt that if they looked upon His face they would not live. Just the opposite was true. Those who looked upon His face had a fuller life.

The fuller life was evidenced by those who gazed upon the face of His Son - for as Jesus said: "He who sees Me sees the Father."

John Paul II's, wise words not to have fear in searching out God, is made clear through the words of the beautiful hymn

"Be not afraid" written by Bob Dufford, SJ. which states: "You shall see face of God and live."

Barbara Rose's book affords us to catch a glimpse of the Face of God, which brings us to a fuller life commitment and which sustains us on our pilgrimage to our heavenly home where this face will be a permanent blessing for us.

I strongly encourage all to read with the eyes of understanding this deeply moving book - to see the Face of God and Live.

Very Reverend Richard J. Whetstone, JCOL
May 17, 1999

PART ONE

YOUR FATHER IS WITH YOU

CHAPTER ONE

I AM THE FATHER
OF ALL MANKIND

At the age of 44, Barbara Rose Centilli began to record what she believed to be the voice of the Eternal Father speaking to her in prayer. Since then, a body of revelations has emerged that many believe to be of the most extraordinary nature, perhaps adding new insight on the First Person of the Holy Trinity.

Barbara Rose was born and raised in Michigan. Except for a few special experiences that she believed to be from God, her life as a mother, grandmother, teacher, and wife were typical of the average American woman of her generation. She received degrees from universities in Michigan and New England, and later taught communications courses and worked as a corporate consultant. But a generous portion of her time was devoted to being a mother to four children and a grandmother to three more.

In the mid 1980's Barbara went from being almost indifferent about her faith to a firm, practicing Catholic who joined a prayer group, taught Catechism, and even became a Eucharistic minister. She also began to develop a silent, steady prayer life that gradually led to her writing prayerful conversations with God the Father in a journal. These conversations took the form of a dialogue, and while she felt God was moving and inspiring her, she believed there was nothing supernatural. These journals were eventually destroyed when a retreat director told her God does not work in this way.

However, in 1996, Barbara again began to record her conversations with the Father. By this time, she noticed the Father's responses to her in prayer were becoming very clear and distinct within her. She could recognize His voice "in her heart and mind." Furthermore, as she reconciled and confronted what was happening to her, she became certain her experiences were not self-induced or imaginative but rather something she had no control over within herself.

The Revelations of the Father

It would not be possible to fully address the extraordinary contents of the revelations given to this soul. Like many revelations, they cover a range of topics and are rich in detail concerning Barbara's interior life with God. However, the essence of the revelations is unmistakable. God the Father was again requesting, as He did with Mother Eugenia Ravasio in 1932, that through His Church all mankind be returned to Him. His children, He told her, must begin to come home to Him at this time. The Father told her that she was to be a special instrument for His messages, a seed to be planted, that would now bring further His Kingdom "on earth as it is in heaven." His children must abandon any fear of Him, He told Barbara, and must know that He is all love and all mercy. Most of all, His plan for the times was at hand and was soon to be fulfilled, and that she had to accept that she had been chosen by Him for this work:

> **Though it may seem that you are alone and abandoned, you are not. The best is yet to come. I have plans for you....Demonstrate your trust by coming to Me in faith, trust, and humility. There is no**

shame in this. Only a wealth of graces-graces, unbound and untethered. That is what grieves you, is that you must let go of the ground beneath you and come to Me in trust. I will catch you in My arms-and never leave you-because you are Mine. Delivered to Me by My Son and Your Mother-to do My will. There is no escape from this, daughter. My will. Embrace it and do not let it frighten you. Remember, you are Mine always and forever; you are dear to Me. (August 15, 1996)

Later, she wrote another extraordinary message in her journal:

Remember, child, all is well within My heart....stop, listen. The crashing of the waves. The pounding of the sea, sound breaking over rocks....THE TIME HAS COME FOR THE RECKONING OF MANKIND -A REUNION WITH ITS FATHER. You have all been away a very long time. The call is on, the crashing and the calling-but to hear the call, broken over the rocks, the hard, hard rocks, you must be in the silence and dark of the night. You've always known this.

I have shown you this symbolism and have shared this with you in our dialogues for many months now. The time has come for you to explain this to My other children. Help them understand that this is the GREATEST HOUR OF MY MERCY. This is the Triumph long awaited for. But so

7

many will be lost without the light of this loving message.

I am the Father of All Mankind. I love each and every one of My children. My heart desires that I live in My children and they in Me. I long to live among My children. The Great Sun amidst so many stars—all glowing with the Love of God. Such glory. Such power. Such wonders await those children who choose to return home now.

Night falls and the storm approaches. My children need to convert, turn toward their Father, and come home. And when they arrive at the threshold of My loving arms, they must say "Yes, Father, I will dance with You in the rhythm and harmony of Your divine will." In this way they will remain with Me always— with and in Me. Not outside Me, separated from Me.

It is all quite simple. Before you took refuge in your Mother's Immaculate Heart. She was truly in My divine will and so in Me and I in her. Now it is time to recognize that in being safely in her heart, you are in Me, your Father. The process, a roadway leading to Me. Mary, your Mother, is in the heart of My Son Who is in My heart—One contained in the Other. How is this possible? Through My Holy Spirit. (Sept. 30, 1997)

On November 30, 1997, the Eternal Father revealed to Barbara the meaning of a dream He had given her and why Our

Lady communicated to her about this dream in another message:

> Where you lay your head is on a bed of roses—each sweet and pure. This pillow of roses is made up of the souls that have sacrificed themselves for the good of all. They have given themselves for this holy purpose. Here you will find your rest, little one.
>
> Roses, roses all, who give themselves to the Father. Each blossoming on the spring of My merciful water. My water of love. Each rose watered by My life-giving water. The water which proceeds through Me, through the heart of My Son and the hands of your loving Mother—graces to bring you home. This is important. Little time remains before I will come and visit My children. I will come to make My abode with them. Prepare them. Make them ready.
>
> A rose must be watered and opens to the sun. Be beautiful as the rose, My children. Open up to your Father. Be all that you were intended to be. Without My saving water, without the warmth and radiance of My sun, you will wither and perish, never to realize what you could have been—My heirs. Now do you understand, Barbara?
>
> The rose on your pillow was for you—it was your own soul. Opened and blossoming in the sun, which is the Father. Yes, daughter, even the rose that has

bloomed will soon die, and so with all My children. But this is the way it must be. You and so many others will send the sweet scent of your offering and consecration to Me—especially on My Feast Day—to the very heavens. Draw Me with this scent. For soon I will come, as I have planned. Draw down My mercy, Barbara. Teach all My children to draw down My mercy. And I will surely, come. Soon, very soon. Time is but a pane of glass that we look through. It is like a transparent sheet of glass. See Me through it." (Nov. 30, 1997)

CHAPTER TWO

CONSECRATE YOURSELVES TO ME

T hrough a series of messages, the Eternal Father communicated to Barbara that the end of an era will dawn upon the world and that these are truly prophetic times. Most significantly, the long awaited Triumph of the Church is about to be fulfilled. This is the "Triumph" Mary promised at Fatima in 1917. And according to the Father's words to Barbara Centilli, it will be completely fulfilled in accordance with His will through two means: *Individual Consecration to God the Father and by the Catholic Church proclaiming a Feast Day in His Name.*

Like the 1932 revelations to Mother Eugenia Ravasio, the Father revealed to Barbara that this request needed to be addressed at this time in salvation history, before the end of the 20th century:

There is not much time, little one. Draw this world into the heavenly paradise of My divine will. Heaven and earth will touch. Bid Me come, and I will come— followed by My Son and the power of My Holy Spirit—to renew the face of the earth. To begin again as in the old ways, I will be present again. And My presence will remain for all times, in all places. I will be

present with and in My children, as I have willed from the beginning of all time.

Come to Me, My little ones. Come back to your Father Who loves you. Night approaches and surely you will be lost. Approach now while there is light. Come by the light. Follow My Son home. He gathers up My children. The sheep are being gathered in—as we speak. Do you understand little one?

The Consecration and Feast Day are the beacon and the means by which My children may approach Me and by which I will come to My children. "THY KINGDOM COME, THY WILL BE DONE ON EARTH AS IT IS IN HEAVEN." Your Mother has prepared for this long and many years. Now is the time. Rest in this knowledge. Your offering has been accepted. In opening the invitation and reading, you have offered it back to Me. Work for the restoration of My children.

FATIMA leads to this time. Fatima leads to Me. The time of the revelry is over. The time of rebellion is over. Make My presence known through the Consecration and Feast Day. I am coming. Prepare yourselves. (November 13, 1997)

On January 12, 1998, the Eternal Father revealed to Barbara more about the meaning of the Miracle of the Sun at Fatima and how the miracle illustrated the consequences of choices, choices mankind must make at this time:

Be at peace, daughter. You have

suffered much for this work I have given you. Put the pen to paper and write. All around you is in the blaze of a recovery from sin. The wind blows but the motion of My Spirit goes undetected. See it in the workings and phenomenon which surround you—and the world at large. These are times steeped in treachery and intrigue. Much is transpiring which My children cannot and may not see. For it is cloaked behind a veil of secrecy and sin. There will be a reprieve, a brief time more before the knowledge of this can no longer be denied. Pray, pray. Pray with your whole heart—given to Me in reparation—and for solace. Understand the gravity of what I say. Much is transpiring—even now. This time is decisive. My children must choose; they must respond now. I weep for them—all the missed opportunities. Fortify them, daughter, with My Consecration and Feast Day.

All is foretold in the Miracle of the Sun (at Fatima) — The pattern of the fabric I have woven is drawn tighter and the image clearer. Do you understand? All the colored threads of the tapestry which is the story of mankind's salvation history, their journey home to Me, is played out on the diorama that is before you. All the answers are there....Help My children see the grand tapestry which is before

them. Watch the threads as they are woven more tightly together. The image comes into clearer focus. The analogy is greater than you thought. Meditate on this. Ponder it in your heart. It (the Miracle of the Sun at Fatima) was more simple than they [My children] thought. A graphic illustration. You were correct in your assumptions about the sun—now follow through on the thought. Why was this shown to My children at that particular time? Meditate on the effects. Harnessing the sun. Harnessing God. For I am energy and light. Consequences–response. Now is the time for choices. Wisely made, based on love. Know Me, My children, before it is too late! I come and I come soon. Know this and be ready. Forgive all those who have offended you. Time is short. And soon petty annoyances, slights, and irritations will no longer matter. I will come to My children in a new way, a powerful way. Sleep now and remain close to My Fatherly heart. (Jan. 12, 1998)

Several months later, the Father revealed to Barbara how all of Mary's work has been leading to this moment in time, His return, and how all can be symbolically understood in the Miracle of the Sun on October 13th, 1917, at Fatima:

My daughter, you must realize by now the tightly woven bond which exists between this devotion to Me and the immediate steps leading up to the Triumph of your Mother's Immaculate Heart. Laid

14

out in the scheme of mankind's salvation history is the end, the ultimate completion of this journey. Through your Mother's fiat, her "Yes," My Son Jesus came into the world to redeem My children, all. Now, the time approaches when this final Triumph will be realized....

Only when I am recognized, loved, and honored by My children—all—will this Triumph be completed. Do you understand?

The return of My children is your Mother's Triumph. All My children must return unhindered to their one true God and Father. Then My Kingdom will have come on earth as it is in Heaven.

This process will be gradual, but IT MUST BEGIN NOW....Each of My children has their role to play in My plan for mankind....Yours to present to the world—now in this time.

I come to My children as was shown in the MIRACLE OF THE SUN. [at Fatima] I come so close to warm you and fill you with My light. Why does this frighten My children? Because they are not ready; they are not prepared. They are not able to see beyond their own preconceptions— their constructions of truth. And the approach of your God without proper preparation as outlined by your Mother is folly indeed. Purification must take place. A cleansing of hearts, bodies, and minds. [I see an image of the Miracle of the Sun—the way the sun's rays seem to color and permeate everything they touch.]

See how I effused all that I touched. See how I chased away the gloom and discomfort. I am light and love. And I bring with Me a power that will transform. All will be transformed in the Lord. I WAS PRESENT AT THE MIRACLE OF FATIMA—in graphic depiction of what could have been and what will be yet.

St. Joseph, My good and tender son, represented the Fatherly arms that hold and behold My Son Jesus—as I desire to hold all of you. The Spirit, My Spirit, was represented in the rays of the sun penetrating all My creation. The miracle was not as great as it could have been. I withdrew from My children as they shrank away in terror from the power and glory of their God. Even then many forget the impact of this experience. Yes, daughter, I am represented in the sun as you see clearly in holy Scripture, My Word. The power of the sun gives life, but it has also been harnessed by man, in aping God, to take life away. LIFE OR CHASTISEMENT. HOW WILL THE POWER OF GOD BE USED?

I wait patiently, oh, so patiently, to enter you and warm your souls in My love. But as with all My gifts, even this has been abused and will be again in chastisement if My little ones do not find their way back home to their Father. At Fatima you saw the options and reactions played out. Approach Me in love and trust and you have nothing to fear. I showed you this at

Fatima. See and believe.

I wish mightily for this devotion to be spread swiftly and without hindrance — this Holy Octave of Consecration to God the Father. Be at peace and know that your Father guides you in your efforts. All you need will be provided in My own way, in My own time. Delight in this gift I give the world. Understand this priceless gift I have placed in your hands. This is what your mother Mary has prepared you so diligently. The precipice is closer than you think, mankind. Approach your Father who will save you as I have written in 1 Sm 3:21. (March 23, 1998)

[1 Sm 3:21-- "And the Lord appeared again at Shiloh for the Lord revealed himself to Samuel at Shiloh by the word of God." (Shiloh was a central shrine to God, sanctified by the presence of the Ark of the Covenant.)]

CHAPTER THREE

THE FEAST IS FOR
MY CHILDREN

T he Holy Octave of Consecration and its Feast Day, the Father revealed to Barbara, was significant in His plan for the new era. Over a period of months, the Father explained the concept of the "Octave" to Barbara, its relevance to the Old Testament times, and its relevance to the future of the Church and all mankind. Barbara came to understand that Christmas and Easter were once celebrated as Octaves and that this Feast would be, in that same tradition.

Indeed, the Father told Barbara how Scripture clearly revealed the concept of an 8-day preparation:

> **The time is ripe! Your purpose will bloom forth with power and My glory. I will work through you. You are very sensitive to My will. You are not comfortable in the world because you were not made for this world....You will fully realize your mission in time. For now, ponder My requests for re-consecration of My Temple. THIS PROCESS TAKES 8 DAYS. Yes, you are right. I am not speaking only of a physical Church, but My living Church and My people individually. LOOK TO SCRIPTURE**

TO BEGIN PREPARATION.

Barbara, the 8 days is significant because it is a purification process. My Tabernacle, My Church, My people have been contaminated. Where darkness is, I cannot be. The darkness must be displaced, swept clean, sunshine and fresh air—housecleaning. TO DO THIS TAKES 8 DAYS OF PREPARATION. ONLY THEN WILL I COME—only then....Look to the Psalms, Jeremiah, Hosea, Wisdom, Revelations....(October 10, 1996)

On February 2, 1997, the Father explained what would be accomplished over the 8-day period:

EIGHT DAYS SIGNIFIES A PERIOD OF TIME MAN LIVES THROUGH AND THEN A TRANSFORMATION OR NEW PERIOD BEGINS. Through these periods, I have saved man many, many times.

Scripture starts out with Noah and the EIGHT on the Ark. Because of those "EIGHT" safely carried in My Ark, mankind was saved, and so it was again and again.

After EIGHT days, through My circumcision covenant, you became My children and were saved. Even My Son Jesus underwent this ritual. Then He became the sign of My Covenant. Through the purification rituals, you were healed and saved from sin.

Through EIGHT days of prayer,

purification, and dedication, I came to be in and with My children.

My Son, on the Feast of Dedication (8-day feast), announced that He and I were One, that I was with you and among you— in Him.

After EIGHT days, I revealed to Peter, James, and John on Mount Tabor who My Son Jesus was—God, My Son. This was transformation and the beginning of a new period.

After EIGHT days, My Son was victorious in saving My children—He conquered sin and death by rising on the EIGHTH day of His Passion Week.

After EIGHT days, Jesus came to His frightened, doubting Apostles to show His Risen Self.

Always, a revelation, a transformation after a period of time. To you, My little one, EIGHT is important. IT POINTS TO A NEW TIME, A NEW TRANSFORMATION WHEN I WILL BE WITH YOU ALL IN A NEW WAY.

You must prepare yourselves for Me to come. YOU MUST PURIFY AND DEDICATE YOUR TEMPLES.

SEE THE "8"--TWO CIRCLES: They are continuous, Barbara. Two perfect circles joined—the beginning and the end, the Alpha and the Omega joined with My children. It is through this Octave that My children are joined with Me. Speak this, Barbara. Show them how this is so. The 8— it is more than a concept, but a visual aid!

You are Mine, little one. Be one with Me. I love you as you do Me. Bring souls, My dearest daughter. This is no light matter. WAKE UP! See Me! I am with you, little one. The "EIGHT"—a perfect harmony of the influx of the Holy Spirit. So be it!!! (March 16, 1997)

As in former times, the Holy Octave of Consecration to God our Father is an eight-day consecration to be celebrated as a whole, culminating with a special feast day in the Church to honor the Father of All Mankind. The actual consecration involves a series of daily prayers, including meditations, a litany, and the praying of a chaplet, all directed to God the Father. (See back of book.)

It must be especially noted that the Father emphasizes to Barbara Centilli that there is to be no separation of the two—the Consecration and its Feast Day. This is because, He says, the **"practical purpose of the Feast (Day) is for My children to consecrate themselves to Me."** The Father further states that **"the Feast does not exist for the purpose of providing Me with a Feast Day on the Church calender. It is what the Feast accomplishes—the return of My children to their Father! This cannot be accomplished with limited and temporary honor given Me at one Mass on one Sunday a year. No, this is much greater than one act....this is the final step toward the new era, a new relationship with their Father and God."**

While much more could be noted, one final point is emphasized. Through the Holy Octave of Consecration and Feast Day, the Father declared to Barbara that this is the fulfillment of what was meant from the beginning. This, He states to her, is to a degree the meaning of the profound words in the Lord's prayer, **"Thy will be done....Thy Kingdom come on earth as it is in Heaven."** It is the long awaited

Triumph of God, promised by so many visionaries.

The Virgin Mary also told Barbara about the coming of her Triumph:

> **Your Father is with you. From His hands comes my Triumph. Through me all the children of God are beckoned and led back home. See the events around you? Do you doubt that the drama unfolds? Each is to play their own part. Truly let it be known that the passing of an era is upon us. As surely as the sun sets, it will also rise. My Son's Passion is seen and felt more clearly in these times. All must carry their cross. Bear up, child. Know that I am always with you. Through the grace of God all will be well for those who bear the light of my Son's Cross.** [She points to the sun and I see a cross embedded in its center.] **See, the earth is left barren, rocky and dry, bones lay bare and scattered. I hold you, daughter, and I promise you this—cherish Me as I have cherished you. Soon the darkness and struggle that separate us will be chased away in the dawning of a new era.**

The Father then added to her some more insight:

> **Barbara, the horn has been sounded. Let those who have ears hear. Yes, there is much clatter and noise that drowns out the music alerting My children and leading them home. They must stop and listen— quietly. And they will hear. It is the cry of**

the Father for His children. Landless and lost they wander. Allow yourselves to be led by your tender mother. Come to Me—only Me— your Father and your God. The drum beat sounds to the rhythm and harmony of My will. Feel the intensity and power of this time. Gather yourselves together to await the coming of your Father. CONSECRATE YOURSELVES TO ME. HONOR ME WITH A FEAST DAY. SHARE WHAT I HAVE GIVEN TO YOU WITH THE WORLD....

Never hesitate when you believe it is My will. Never. Proceed. Move forward always toward Me, your Father. There is no fault or danger in this, only My Fatherly embrace. Come to Me, My children. And watch as My glory ascends in this new day. The presence of your God is with you. Of this there will be no doubt. Faith and confidence, My little ones. Your trials will soon be over and we shall begin again. Approach Me. Choose Me in these times.

CHAPTER FOUR

IT IS I, YOUR FATHER
AND YOUR GOD

The Father spoke to Barbara about many other subjects. These revelations were also extraordinary, especially a message and vision given concerning what the world will be like after a certain, terrible but purifying event of God's justice:

[I saw a flat area on the far side of the mountains. There are buildings. They seem to be in ruins and smoldering. I ask My Father where all the people are.]

They have fled the ruins of what once was, as will you all, once at a time in the not too distant future. The ruins are uninhabitable, little one. My children can no longer survive where they once lived, how they once lived. The choice will no longer be theirs. Where they once lived, how they once lived can be no more. My children can no longer survive in the culture "they" have created. (April 6, 1998)

Just as fascinating was the Father's words to Barbara concerning Judith and her times in ancient Israel. It is a story the Father told her that foreshadows the coming Triumph:

It is Mother's Day. I love and honor my mother Mary and my own mother and grandmothers.

Father, I just read the story of Judith. The people of Israel were going to be destroyed by a stronger pagan power. They gave God five days to save them or they were going to surrender to survive. Judith, a chaste widow, prayed to God and said they should not try God with limits. She also said they must be patient and humble and that God sometimes chastises His children for their own good and this is how they should look at it. Judith cuts Holofernes' head off and then when the "sun rises," the Hebrews dress for battle so the enemy will react (but the enemy panics after discovering that their leader has been decapitated). The sun rising is the signal to begin the deceptive offensive–after Judith had laid the groundwork for victory. The sun rising was the sign, the time, to begin their offensive.

Father, what do You wish to tell me on this night? I love You; I adore You; I worship You, my Father.

Be at peace, My little one. Oh, My daughter, look to Judith for a true picture of what will be in the world and for each of My children. What did you learn?

I see the symbolism of the rising sun as a signal or catalyst for action by Your children–in their fight against their adversary. I believe I see Judith prefiguring Our Lady in "crushing the head" of the adversary.

Man's ways are not My ways, daughter. Judith knew this. She remained close to Me in the quiet and seclusion of her upper chamber. Did she not caution My children against testing Me—setting time limits for My action or response? She knew

My children can approach Me only in humility and that I chastise those I love—allowing them to be overtaken and defeated when they wander outside My will. And do I not come to their defense when they choose to remain in My will? Such a simple formula for peace, is it not? Humble submission to My will. And the defeat of the adversary comes through the hands of a woman. She went stealthily into the enemy's camp, adorned in all her beauty and splendor, feigning betrayal of her own people, using wiles to combat wiles, and committing the fatal act of removing the head of the enemy.

Think on this, little one. The enemy's head must be crushed and My children must act when the sun rises—and I will do the rest. The enemy will flee in disorder and great distress. For the head of their initiative is no more, has been crushed, beheaded, separated from the body—by the woman. A woman beautiful and chaste—a woman given solely to the Creator—her God and Father.

She knew what was needed and so should you all. Your Mother comes in these times to tell you over and over, calling you unceasingly. But still, so many do not listen. Who will be ready to put on their armor when the sun rises? It is I, your Father and your God. And I will come on the heels of your Mother's great Triumph. Who will be ready? Who will be awake to see the sun rising in a new dawn, a new day?

27

The Prodigal Son spent his inheritance on harlots—lust, a counterfeit of love. The wedding feast of the Lamb and His Bride awaits all those who wish to return home and who can overcome those things outlined in the revelation of the Apostle John. Look to those things, daughter.

The Chaplet encapsulates the response of the Prodigal Son. This is good. Now what must be overcome on the journey home?

Suit up for the battle. There must be charity between My children and love between each child and Me, your Father. False doctrine and prophets must be rejected. My children must feel passion in their love of their Father, and they must complete all the necessary work needed for their journey home.

What awaits them? Life! I am Life. And that is where it all began and where it all must return. Do you understand, little one? No death, no lies, no counterfeits. Only the truth of life in God your Father. I await you all patiently. I see you yet far off and I am beginning to run toward you, arms outstretched and a heart that beats out a song of great relief and tremendous rejoicing. My children are returning home.

They are being restored to their Father and their God. Your Mother acts to protect and defend you in these times. Be at peace and know that all will be well in the Lord!

Raphael says: **Praise His holy Name!**

Our Mother Mary says: **Through their**

prayers, my children can draw down the mercy of God. Tell them. Through your prayers and in conforming to God's will—you remain in the heart of our Father. Protected and cherished always. Choose, my children! I cajole and nudge, but you must make the choice of your own free will. All has been laid out in Holy Scripture. Open your eyes, ears, and heart—and believe! The Day of the Lord is at hand. The Peace of the Lord is with you—remember that always. Now you, too, must be about your Father's business.

Reading: Is. 13—"...Howl ye, for the day of the Lord is near: it shall come as destruction from the Lord....For this I will trouble the heaven: and the earth shall be moved out of her place, for the indignation of the Lord of hosts, and for the day of his fierce wrath...."

Reading: Judith 8—"...This is not a word that may draw down mercy, but rather that may stir up wrath and enkindle indignation....You have set a time for the mercy of the Lord, and you have appointed him a day, according to your pleasure...." (May 11, 1998)

CHAPTER FIVE

MY KINGDOM

On May 12, 1988, the Father explained to Barbara about what it really means for a king to have a kingdom, and how the world needs to be for "His Kingdom to come." Again, the following entry is from her journal:

Dearest Father:

Father, if it is Your will, would You offer us some insight on Acts 1:6-7: "Lord wilt thou at this time restore again the kingdom to Israel? But he said to them: It is not for you to know the times or moments, which the Father hath put in his own power." Jesus said it is not for us to know the time or moment of the restoration of the Kingdom. Is there any connection between the restoration of the Kingdom to Israel and the Holy Octave of Consecration?

If it pleases You to respond to this, Father, your daughter is listening.

Be at Peace, My daughter: Let the gentle calm of the day's end settle over you. My Kingdom. What is My Kingdom? A kingdom is something a King reigns over. But it is more. It is a place where he lives. A place that he protects. A place where he maintains peace and dispenses justice. A good king is just and fair and is loved by his people. Ideally, a kingdom exists in

harmony and affords the people security and happiness. A king should be honored and respected by his people. All these things are true of a kingdom, are they not, Barbara Rose?

Yes, ideally, Father.

You ask Me if the restoration of the Kingdom to Israel is somehow connected to the Holy Octave of Consecration. First of all, a king should be present to his people, not only to afford them protection but to give them hope and heart. Do I truly dwell with My children? Do they see and hear Me in their lives? Secondly, do My children honor and respect Me? How so, My daughter? Thirdly, do My children feel security and happiness in the realm they now live in? Perhaps on a superficial level.

For a kingdom to come, My children must acknowledge their king. They must recognize that there is indeed a kingdom. The Kingdom of God is not forced upon My children. They must choose to enter it. They must choose to return home to their Father.

So many images: Father and Paradise, King and Kingdom, the New Jerusalem. What does all this mean?

Expressed in simple terms, I speak of My children returning home to Me. Where I am, so is Heaven, so is Paradise, so is the New Jerusalem.

As I have explained to you before, little

one, the Kingdom will not come from without but from within.

How can it ever come if My children refuse to see it, acknowledge it? Even more, they must want it.

How many of My children acknowledge that it exists? How many bid it come? How can they? They have no knowledge or belief in it.

When the cutting edge of truth slices through the illusion that is the world, those who are not prepared will have difficulty in adjusting to the light which will penetrate powerfully into each and every soul.

Who will welcome this Kingdom? Who will embrace this Kingdom? Who will battle and overcome for this Kingdom?

Remember what I have told you— the children of God can have no kingdom restored to them, O Israel, until they know, love, and honor their Creator and Father. Then and only then will the Kingdom truly settle into the hearts of My children and My Kingdom will be realized on earth.

Stages and degrees have been involved in the coming of this Kingdom— the restoration of the children of God to their Father. Now is the time that it comes into clearer and clearer relief—toward final realization.

Do you need to ask, Barbara Rose? Truly, in your heart you know the answer. You have outlined the path of My children's journey home—culminating in an Octave

Consecration and Feast Day. Can you not see? The prodigal children will at last have found their Father. They will celebrate with joy. For in finding Him, they are no longer lost. Having been dead, they are now come to life.

As I requested an 8-day feast in Old Testament times, so now My children respond to My desire to be known, loved, and honored at this time, in this way. And as with the final day of assembly, this Consecration Feast Day will serve to regather ALL My children. The spirit will move mightily in this effort.

My children's response—so sweet and simple: "I love You, Father, and I give myself to You." And I will come to dwell with you and I will be your God and you will be my people—I am your Father and you are My children. And once you have found your way home, you will look around you and realize that you are loved and protected for all time. For you are now in the Kingdom. The Kingdom has come and it dwells in you as you dwell in it. Do you comprehend what I am saying to you, daughter?

My children must acknowledge My existence. They must see that I am truly their Father. They must choose to leave the world of sin and disobedience and come to Me—in humility and trust. And I will shower them with such tender love as they have never before experienced or imagined.

Do you see now how the Holy Octave of

Consecration to God Your Father leads to the restoration of the Kingdom to Israel—My children?

I believe so, Father.

There should be joy and celebration. As in the return of the Prodigal Son!

[Reading: Gal 4:1-7—"Now I say, as long as the heir is a child, he differeth nothing from a servant, though he be lord of all; but is under tutors and governors until the time appointed by the father: so we also, when we were children, were serving under the elements of the world. But when the fulness of the time was come, God sent his son, made of a woman, made under the law: that he might redeem them who were under the law: that we might receive the adoption of sons. And because you are sons, God hath sent the Spirit of his Son into your hearts, crying: Abba, Father. Therefore now he is not a servant, but a son. And if a son, an heir also through God."]

And so, daughter, from servitude to sonship—and now is time for the children of God to return home. Thus will the Kingdom of God be restored to Israel—My children, all.

A parting thought, daughter. The Prodigal Son, by choice, returned to his father. By choice, always by choice.

Sleep in My peace, little one.

(May 12, 1998)

35

CHAPTER SIX

I FEEL ALL THAT MY CHILDREN FEEL

The Father also explained to Barbara how Abraham's sacrifice of Isaac and Christ's sacrifice on the Cross are mystically connected, and how He, the Father of All Mankind, suffers daily in this manner still:

> Now as to your question regarding Abraham and these times you live in— these precarious times. Have I not shown you how My Fatherly heart breaks from My children's suffering? Each one, daughter, is in a sense offered on the pyre of sacrificial offering to Me. And in their sacrificial offering I am united with them in a way that goes beyond compassion or pity. Yes, it is true, that I feel ALL that My children feel. But do I not also feel, in addition to the pain, the anguish of a Father who must witness the sacrificial pain and suffering of each and every one of My little ones? Comprehend what this means. I cannot eradicate the suffering. I cannot take away the sacrifice. Each must follow in the steps of their Brother and Lord God—My Son Jesus.

So I have ordained it. Did I Myself not suffer, die, and be buried in and with My Son? I was the agent and victim, Father and child.

But, Father, why is this necessary? If it grieves you so, why must Your children suffer to be reunited and restored to You? Couldn't there have been any other way?

No, little one, My rose, because each human life is precious and bestowed with free will. Only in this way can My children be FREE to choose their Father, to love their Father.

And to draw the human spirit back toward its origin, its Creator, its Father, there must be a path of purgation and purification. And so the sacrificial wood of suffering, whether it be the flames of offering or the suffering of the Cross, all leads to Me, the Father.

Now, how is this related to these times and the Holy Octave of Consecration to God our Father? I am providing the wood of sacrifice, the means of sacrificial offering through the eight days of Consecration and My Feast Day. In this way all is subsumed back into the Father. All is brought back into My Fatherly heart which is torn asunder until all is restored. Do you understand?

Yes, I think so, Father. So *The Holy Octave of Consecration to God our Father* is like the pyre in Abraham's Old Testament story and the Cross of Jesus in the New Testament.

Daughter, this gift to My children in this time will send sacrificial smoke ascending to Heaven—a final connection between the Father and His children. In this way, all will eventually be completed, restored to Me—the Father of All Fathers. Through the example of My sacrificial offering, My children resemble their Father in all things.

The eight flames upon the Cross, daughter! Remember this image. [I see the Cross with eight candles lit and the smoke from the flames ascending into heaven.] The offering on the wood of My Son's Cross— the bridge home to Me, your one true God and Father, sacrificial smoke ascending to Heaven.

Be with Me as I am with you. Be in Me as I am in you. This is how I will come to My little ones, all. I await the response of My children, given in offering to Me, as I have offered Myself for them.

Now go in My gentle and merciful peace played out so powerfully in these times.

Reading: Gen. 42:33-38: *...You will bring down my gray hairs with sorrow to hell"* [Jacob's lament over possibly losing another child.]

The Father's explicit revelations of all that is unfolding in both the spiritual and physical realms is especially revealing. The Eternal Father told Barbara on July 23, 1998, that the culture we live in is toxic to our souls and leading us to ruin. Only He, He told

Barbara, can save mankind:

Everyone I know is having serious problems—especially with their children. Lord, why can't people see that the culture is destroying the children?

The culture has become toxic, daughter.

Father, if we agree that the culture is toxic, what is the answer? What can we do? Please tell me, Father. I know You want us to come home to You and You want us to know, love, and honor You—but there is something still lacking in what You ask of us—those children who say "Yes" to this. Father, do we stay in and fight or do we separate and leave. This is not entirely clear. But please help me understand.

I am with You, Father, and I am listening.

Barbara, My Daughter:
The result of My children's choices is indeed the culture you are now living in. It is replete with every kind of menace and defilement imaginable. And what was unacceptable, unthinkable, even one generation ago, is now commonplace, has now been legislated into law. The law, little one. Laws that legalize corruption and sin. Laws that violate the laws of God—My truth, My will.

How can this be? Because My children have abandoned Me. They think of Me no more. To them, I am nothing more than a legend, a myth. That is why, Barbara Rose, My presence is no longer perceived or desired by My children. Why? Because for

them I no longer exist. I never did. I have been explained away and banished to the past.

But some yet remain in My truth, in My will. And for these, existence has become very difficult, if not impossible. The disease of your culture has spread and is out of control—its victims most often are the children.

This you know, child. But your question was "What are we to do, Father?"

I repeat to you again: know, love, and honor Me. By raising up this Standard (The Holy Octave of Consecration to God our Father and Feast Day), many [of My children]—more than you imagined—will rally toward it. And here is your strength for what yet lies ahead. There is strength in My little Remnant, the ranks of which will swell as more and more children are awakened from their sleep. Anesthetized so long. Not conscious of the state of darkness that has developed subtly, but, oh, so swiftly. But it is here, the darkness I speak of, and it is time to move toward the light. The light of your Lord God and Father.

Follow where the Light of God leads you, daughter. Follow My Light and you will find Me—waiting to welcome you home.

Now sleep in My peace.

Reading: Dn. 7:25—"And he [the antichrist] shall think himself able to change times

41

and laws." (April 11, 1998)

[Editor's Note: All of the published revelations of the Eternal Father to Barbara Centilli are contained in the books: *Seeing with the Eyes of the Soul: Volumes I, II, and III*, published by St. Andrew's Productions. See the back of this book for further information on how to order these books.]

PART TWO

THE FACE OF THE FATHER

CHAPTER SEVEN

CALLED BY THE FATHER

AN INTERVIEW WITH BARBARA CENTILLI

The following is an in-depth, extensive and revealing interview with Barbara Centilli. It's candor and insight are most revealing of who our Father is and how He awaits our return to His protective arms.

Q. *Barbara, tell us how your devotion to God our Father began?*

A. The first real memory I have of devotion to our Father took place when I was a child. I came home from school one day and I was very sick. Both my parents worked, and on this particular day, my dad came home first. He took me to the doctor who gave me a shot of penicillin. The next memory I have is looking up at my dad and telling Him I couldn't breathe. I felt as if I was dying. I realized in that instant that he (my earthly father) couldn't save me—only my Heavenly Father could. This was quite an epiphany for me. I learned later that I had gone into anaphylactic shock and could have died.

After that, as I was growing up, the Catholic school I

attended focused primarily on Jesus and Mary. As an adult, I never really thought about or prayed to God our Father until I read a book about God the Father several years ago. I remember that it seemed too good to be true. For the first time, God our Father seemed like a real person—an extraordinarily wonderful and approachable person. From that time on, I felt close to our Father. It was an invitation to love Him and be loved by Him that I couldn't resist.

Later, I became involved with an Apostolate that was spreading devotion to God our Father. During this period, I would regularly walk around our neighborhood block and say the Rosary. One particular day at dusk (which I realized later was seven days before the first Sunday of August that year), I heard a voice say, "Look up!" After arguing with myself that this must be my imagination, I heard it again. When I finally looked up, I didn't see anything out of the ordinary. It was a normal neighborhood with houses and cars, etc. The only thing that caught my eye were footlights leading up a pathway. I couldn't imagine why anyone would be telling me to look at footpath lights. Then I heard, "Count the lights." I counted eight lights.

I had no knowledge of what this meant or why this would be important. I had no affinity for numbers nor did I attach any special significance to them. I didn't know what to do or where to go for answers. When I got home I went to the Holy Scriptures (which I was only superficially familiar with) and I began to read from beginning to end. Almost immediately, I began to recognize the significance of the number eight (or octave). It was for me a startling revelation. After that, one thing providentially happened after another and I began writing my conversations with our Father down in my prayer journal.

Q.   *Why do you think you were being called by the Father?*

A.   If we were chosen to do God's work based on uncommon sanctity, I would not be a likely candidate. If anything, I am a typical woman who was born at the mid-point of this century, grew up in America in the 50's and 60's, went to college and had a family. I have the same weaknesses as everyone else and have made many of the poor choices and mistakes common to every human being. Sometimes I think of myself as the "poster child for prodigal children."

Q.   *Has God the Father ever appeared to you, as in an apparition?*

A.   I have never seen any corporeal visions. I see our Father in prayer, in my heart. These experiences are very real, very touching, very powerful, and very memorable.

Q.   *How long have these experiences been going on?*

A.   I began hearing the voice of our Father interiorly while I was writing a prayer journal during an Ignatian retreat in the mid-1990's. I was advised to stop listening to the voice of God by the retreat director, but experienced the voice again strongly on that July day when I was told to "Look up!" After, I learned that this experience occurred on the feast of St. Ignatius. I again began writing down my dialogues with our Father in my prayer journal.

Q.   *Tell us how you hear His voice? In your heart or ears?*

A.   I do not hear our Father's voice audibly through my physical senses, my ears. Rather, I hear His voice in my heart. It is different than an imaginative voice. Sometimes it comes unexpectantly. Sometimes I hear His voice while I am actively involved with my own thought processes. In other words, the two things can occur simultaneously. Often, He will repeat things if I hesitate to write them down. But He never forces me. The dialogue is always consensual.

Q.   *Were you afraid at first?*

A.   I was not "afraid." Our Father's voice is never frightening. I would better describe my reaction as confused and concerned. I never wanted to be mislead or to mislead others. This was my constant prayer to our Father. For a long time, I questioned what was happening to me. I agonized over it. But so many providential things happened related to the dialogue. And the Scripture readings our Father gave me were so closely related to the dialogues. The content was so far beyond anything I could have imagined. In fact, if I try to replicate our Father's words, I cannot. I am unable to simulate His content and style.

I think it is human to doubt this type of experience. And certainly I did. I needed to have our Father demonstrate their authenticity and reassure me over and over again—which He did.

Q.   *How often does He speak to you? Where at?*

A.   My spiritual experiences include epiphanies and dialogue. Epiphanies come as powerful and

48

unexpected insight—any time and any place. Usually, they occur during the day when I am active and take me totally by surprise. These are communicated to me as ideas rather than as a voice. The dialogues usually occur in a much more structured environment. I pray the Rosary or chaplet and follow this with an entry in my prayer journal. Our Father then speaks to me and a dialogue occurs. When I dialogue, I take time to quiet myself, usually when my family is gone during the day or when they are asleep at night.

These dialogues would take place whenever I sat down to pray and journal. Sometimes when my life was unusually hectic, several days would pass between dialogues. Sometimes, when I felt the need, I would dialogue more than once a day.

I felt that our Father was always with me—especially during dialogues. At times, I would just sit in the Presence of our Father; other times I was lead only to a reading. There were several times of crisis or illness when I spoke to our Father and I heard His voice separate from the more formal prayer journaling.

I feel our Father is always with me and all His children and that He is available to us whenever we need Him or He needs to communicate something to us. I find myself thinking of and talking to our Father throughout the day.

Q.   *Do you record all your conversations?*

A.   I record only the dialogues in my formal prayer journal. If there is something our Father wants to speak to me about, I will feel a strong prompting to do this. It usually occurs when I have gone several days without journaling due to family obligations. When this happens, I try to journal so that it is written down. I also attempt to include epiphanies in the journal.

I often find myself talking to our Father throughout my busy day, asking Him to help me, commenting on something that has happened, etc. Many times our Father will tell me to have peace or that He loves me and He is with Me. This happens outside formal journaling, usually when I am having some sort of difficulty. This is not recorded in the journal.

Q. *You once said you were advised that God doesn't speak to His children like that. Tell us what happened with the priest who told you this and why you destroyed the original messages.*

A. Several years ago, during a retreat, I was instructed by a priest to begin writing a meditative prayer journal. During this journaling process, I began to hear what I believed to be the voice of our Father within me and to experience interior visions. When I spoke to the priest about this, he told me that God doesn't communicate with us this way, He explained that we should operate by faith only, be highly suspicious of experiences like this, and that we shouldn't desire to hear God's voice or to have visions. This advice disturbed and concerned me so much that I destroyed all my journals.

This saddened me because for the first time in my life, I had felt very, very close to God. The dialogues created an intimacy between myself and God that hadn't existed before. I found that I was relating to Him in a personal, not impersonal manner. I found that I missed

Him and felt a tremendous loss. Our Father became the focus of My Life, and after destroying the journals and feeling that I could never dialogue with our Father again, I felt desolate and very empty.

After the retreat, I continued to recite formal prayers, but I felt our Father drawing me back to Himself—He didn't seem to want an impersonal, superficial relationship, He wanted something different. I felt that He wanted me to speak directly to Him and that, likewise, He wanted to speak directly to me.

After the experience with the eight lights, I began journaling again. I felt our Father wanted an intimate relationship not only with me—but with all of us. I have come to understand that our Father doesn't want one-way communication, with us talking "at" Him. Rather, He wants us to listen for His voice and see Him in His Creation (especially in each other)—to see and hear Him in our soul.

CHAPTER EIGHT

IN THE PRESENCE
OF THE FATHER

Q. *How would you describe the voice of God the Father?*

A. Our Father's voice is the voice of a man—not old, not young, but at the prime of life. It has energy and power—but extraordinary tenderness and compassion. His voice elicits love, not fear. Sometimes His voice is commanding, but never angry. It is not flat and sterile, but lyrical and passionate—passionate with love for His children.

Q. *Have you seen the Father in visions? Tell us about the most extraordinary vision you have had.*

A. Yes, frequently during dialoguing and sometimes after Communion I see our Father interiorly. I don't believe I can single out one vision. What is most memorable is that I am in the intimate presence of our Father. It may be on a mountaintop watching the sun rise, in a meadow as He calls His children home, near a campfire telling me we must prepare for a battle, or in a place deep in my heart. But the theme is always the same. He greatly desires that all His children come home to Him and that this time is important—we must choose.

Q. *What exactly does He look like? Does He look old? Does He have a long white beard? How was He dressed?*

A. As with His voice, our Father is neither young nor old. He is in the prime of Life. His hair is dark, slightly wavy, and slightly longer than shoulder length. He has no beard or mustache. His eyes are brilliant blue. His clothing has never really seemed important to me. His eyes and smile are what draws my attention.

Q. *Does God the Father seem happy or harsh?*

A. Our Father has never seemed harsh. He seems serious and concerned, sometimes even sad about His children. This causes Him great suffering. Many times, though, He smiles, very, very gently and lovingly. He also has a sense of humor and when I've been terribly sad, He has tried to make me laugh or smile.

When I was discerning *The Holy Octave of Consecration to God Our Father*, I would occasionally have uncertainties and He would show me the "8" in the most unexpected places. And I would smile and even laugh at the strange, mysterious, and even sometime humorous ways of our Father.

Q. *Does God the Father ever get angry in your conversations with Him?*

A.   No, I can't say "angry." Concerned, serious, and powerful are how I would describe it–like a parent who has lost their children and is frantically looking for them.

Q.   *What message is the most significant one, in your opinion, that really revealed Him to you?*

A.   I don't really view the dialogues as separate messages but the ongoing unfolding of one unified message. The message is this–God is our one true Father and we are His true children. Our Father has been waiting for His prodigal children to return home. These are critical times and we must make a free-will choice–to choose God our Father and His Love, Mercy, and Holy Will. This period is special, and perhaps soon this time of tremendous grace will be over. It is God's plan that His children know, love, and honor Him by consecrating themselves to Him and by celebrating His feast day (*The Holy Octave of Consecration to God our Father*).

This is directly tied into our Lady's Triumph and the coming of our Father's Kingdom on earth as it is in Heaven. We have not begun to understand yet our inheritance as the children of God.

Q.   *Have you experienced any miracles with Him?*

A.   There have been, what I consider, private miracles and ongoing providential occurrences. But my love for our Father, the work that has been done, and His Presence with me are more miraculous than anything I could ever ask for.

Q.   *Have you seen Mary?*

A.   Yes. To me, she looks very much as she is represented in the Fatima statue. She is very loving and maternal. There is nothing to fear from her. Our Lady comes to me when I am sick or weary—she is our true Mother. In fact, she seems more my mother than my earthly mother, whom I love dearly.

Q.   *Have you seen Jesus?*

A.   Yes. Often, I see Him on the Cross. He is always with our Lady.

Q.   *What role has Mary played in this plan?*

A.   Our Lady has always appeared as a comforter and one who gives advice. My understanding is that she will triumph when the children of God return to their Father. This will occur when she crushes the head of the seducer who wants nothing more than to separate us from our Father.

Q.   *Have you seen angels?*

A.   During prayer I have seen angels as I see our Father— in my heart. Raphael, especially, has played an important role in this work.

Q.   *Have you been to Heaven, Hell, or Purgatory? Have you been told about these eternal destinations?*

A.   No, I have not seen Heaven, Purgatory or Hell. In the dialogues, our Father primarily stresses His desire that all His children return to Him. I know the possibility of His children not finding their way home exists, though, because our Father is extremely concerned that they do find their way home. He tells me that it will be very difficult when His light is withdrawn—when this special period of grace ends. I don't believe I needed to "see" the actual suffering of Purgatory or the horror of Hell to believe that they exist. His loving and passionate concern that none of His children be separated from Him is what thoroughly convinced me.

Q. *Have any Saints come to you?*

A. During the dialogues I have seen young David several times. He has always beckoned me to follow him up a hill or mountain. At the top was a new church or temple. I wasn't allowed to go in yet, but we admired it from the outside. David seemed very excited. Our Father has spoken to me about Abraham, Isaac, Mary Magdalene, Ruth, Judith, etc. I have also had a recurring vision during the dialogues which involves Peter and the Apostles.

Q. *Have you seen Satan? Demons?*

A. At the beginning of my spiritual experiences in the late 1980's, I had a dream that was more real than if I had been awake. In that dream, I was in a courtyard. Across the courtyard was a man—a very attractive man. I was drawn to him and seemed to run toward him. But as I got closer, he became more and more horrid looking, uglier and more hideous than anything I could describe. He was so horrifying that my heart seized up and I began to experience what I feel was a heart attack and death. I didn't know what to do and so I prayed the *Hail Mary*. I had to pray very slowly, as I could barely breathe or move from the crushing pain. But the pain remained and I frantically grasped for something to save me. I then began to say the *Our Father* prayer. Each word came out agonizingly slow. By the time I got to the last word, the pain eased up enough that I could breathe better, and I woke up. I was shaking and terrified for hours after that.

At first, I was confused about why I wasn't able to stop with the *Hail Mary*, and I had to go on to the *Our Father* prayer. I believe now that the hideous being I experienced was Satan, and I was being shown that our Lady always takes us to our Father who ultimately "delivers us from evil."

Q.   *Has our Father spoken about the Sacraments?*

A.   Yes, I have come to understand and appreciate our Father's true Presence in the Holy Sacraments. He has said that we should approach Him through the Sacraments and the devotion He has given us. Our Father has explained that the Church with its Sacraments was designed so that we could become "real" children of God, of His own being and image. Mary shapes and leads us, so Jesus may dwell in us. In this way, our Father is with us. This is His most fervent desire. I was also told that the "Day of the Lord" approaches and that we must all prepare ourselves in body, mind, and soul.   We need to purify ourselves, availing ourselves of the Holy Sacraments and preaching the good news. Our Father explained that a time would come when the Sacraments would be administered by a scant few, but that the Church would not die....a new time and new traditions were coming.

CHAPTER NINE

THE FATHER REVEALS
HIS PLAN

Q. *The Father speaks to you of "Mercy with Justice."*
Tell us what you believe this means.

A. My understanding is that the words "mercy" and "justice" are not antithetical—they are not oppositional or contradictory. Instead, because of the condition of the world, our Father's justice – in correcting what's wrong, making things right, placing us back in sync with His Will— is, in fact, merciful. Without His "merciful justice," we would completely destroy ourselves and separate ourselves from God eternally.

Q. *The Father said to you, "The time has come for a reunion with Him." What will be this reunion? How will it occur?*

A. Our Father wants all His children to come together in peace. He wants us all to come home to Him. The only way these two things can and will occur is when we individually and collectively embrace God as our true Father and we recognize our inheritance as the children of God. Only then will we have the Peace of God. I also believe He is giving us a means for this reunion through *The Holy Octave of Consecration to God our Father*.

Q.   *Are these events in Scripture? Are prophecies being fulfilled here, in your opinion?*

A.   Yes, I believe they are being fulfilled. From the early days of the dialogue, our Father has always drawn me to particular readings in Holy Scripture which I believe highlight, support, or clarify the dialogue. Many of the readings have come from the Old Testament, especially the prophetic books.

The selected passages many times deal with chastisement. But they also promise restoration. Several dialogues and readings have specifically referred to the anti-christ and end times—especially how they relate to our breaking God's laws and creating our own laws and idols.

Q.   *This plan, can it also be delayed, canceled, or mitigated?*

A.   Our Father has always said this is a special time of "choice." Our choices are directly related to consequences. Recently, He said we can "tremble in fear or tremble with love of Him." I also understand that when He does come to us, the state of our preparedness (based on our choices) will have a great deal to do with how we undergo the transformation that will take place.

Q.   *How are we, as the Father said it to you, all prodigal children? Tell us about your vision of the passage in the Bible on this subject.*

A.   One day while dialoguing, I saw the Holy Scriptures
       opened to the middle—to the Parable of the Prodigal
       Son. Then I saw the Book of Genesis at the Beginning
       of the Bible and the Book of Revelation at the end.
       Our Father helped me understand that the entire Bible
       and our salvation history were about this one parable
       and it has to do with each and every one of us—
       individually and collectively.

       From the time of our first parents, every single human
       being (with the exception of Jesus and Mary) has left
       the home of our Father through choice. Our only
       purpose for existing is to find our way back home to our
       Father through our free-will choice to return and by
       saying "Yes" to His Holy Will.

Q.   *Has the Father spoken to you about the Pope? Have
       you had any visions of the Pope? Will the Pope be
       martyred or go into exile?*

A.   I have had visions of the Holy Father being in danger.
       He would fall and there would be darkness in the
       sanctuary, and that then we must move stealthily in this
       night.

Q.   *Has the Father spoken about His son, Jesus, and the
       Redemption?*

A.   My understanding is that our Father loves us so much,
       He wants us home with Him forever. Since we left His
       house (Paradise) to wander, lost, He sent His Son
       Jesus to redeem us so that we could return and then
       lead us back home. Jesus shows us the way home and

reveals the Truth that God is our Father. Through, with, and in Him, we find our inheritance—eternal Life with our Father.

Q.   *Your messages are often accompanied by Scripture quotes. Why is this? Tell us about the meaning of the verses given to you to read.*

A.   In the early days of the dialogue, I reasonably questioned the authenticity of what was happening to me. I asked our Father for a sign. Each time I did this, He would draw me to a Scripture passage. For me, this was miraculous because I am not a Biblical expert, nor have I memorized the Bible chapter and verse. I would either hear the biblical citation, see it visually, or I would be lead to open Scripture, lay my hands on the open page and "feel" the passage.

These quotes almost always compliment, support, and clarify what I have been given in dialogue. Sometimes, however, they deal with preceding or succeeding dialogue. This can only be appreciated by reading and studying the dialogue as a whole. The Scripture readings, when taken as a whole, focus primarily on God's children rebelling, turning away from Him, and leaving home, as well as our Father's merciful chastisements, the restoration of the Temple, and the coming of the New Jerusalem. The theme of vigilance and preparedness for battle are also included.

Q.   *We are, the Father said, "Living in a grace-filled period." Is this the same as Divine Mercy?*

A.   I believe Jesus told Sr. Faustina that a period of Mercy would proceed a period of Justice. And that it was important to respond now, during this period of Mercy. Similarly, in what our Father is relating to me, I understand that this is a special and critical period in mankind's salvation history. This is a time of choice. How is it grace-filled? I believe that through our Lady, our Father is releasing untold graces to soften our hearts and enlighten us so that we accept the Truth that God is our Father, we are His children, and that ultimately we need to be reunited with Him.

Finally, based on the dialogues, I do not believe that this period will last forever—it will eventually end. Our Father has used the word "soon" several times in reference to this. He has said that after the Light has been withdrawn, it will be very, very difficult for those children who are still lost and wandering to find their way home. He is very insistent on this point, and this seems to concern Him very much.

Q. *The Father has spoken to you about the Divine Family. What is the Divine Family?*

A. Our Father has used this term several times during the dialogue. I don't think any human can fully grasp what this means. But my understanding is that the Holy Trinity is relational; it is a family: the Father, His Son, and the Spirit of Love that flows between them. By virtue of Jesus' human and divine nature, His mother Mary is drawn into this Divine Family—she is the Mother of God. Through Mary and in Jesus, we, likewise, are brought into the Heart of our Father. We have the overwhelming privilege of being children of God.

This is not to say that Mary or mankind are part of the Trinity. Rather, we are children of God through Mary and in Jesus and the Holy Spirit. This, I believe, is what our Father means when he refers to the Divine Family.

CHAPTER TEN

CONSECRATION TO OUR FATHER

Q.   *The Father has spoken to you about chapels that are 8X8X8. Can you tell what He wants? Can anyone build them? Will the Father be there in a special way?*

A.   I believe the reference to chapels is both symbolic and literal. 8X8X8 would typically designate height, width, and depth. We can only assume, then, that the chapels are intended to be built physically. However, no exact measurement is given (feet, inches, etc.). Therefore, the proportions would remain constant but the actual size could vary.

Our Father mentioned "chapels" (plural), and so we can also assume that there is to be more than one huge Church. These chapels would, I believe, be places where we could better know, love, and honor our Father. Most importantly, however, I see these chapels symbolizing a new way of life centered around our Father. In other words, our Father would be the central figure in our lives, in our culture, in our world. These chapels represent a new relationship between God and His children. In a sense, they represent our own souls–temples of the Holy Spirit.

THE FACE OF THE FATHER

Lastly, I see the chapels as symbolic of the "Church" as a whole. I believe it is our Father's desire that all His children be reunited and that they know, love, and honor Him. Then He will be with us in a truly new way.

Interestingly, 8X8X8, provides us with three numbers of eight. Three signifies the Holy Trinity, but it also refers to the triad of knowing, loving, and honoring our Father. And the number eight itself represents the Holy Octave of Consecration to God Our Father and the coming of a new era.

Q.   *What is the meaning behind the ejaculation, "I love you, Father, and I give myself to You?" This seems to be a prayer that is a shift from "reparation" to "restoration."*

A.   This ejaculation accomplishes several things. First, in saying it from the heart, we are addressing and, thereby, acknowledging God as our Father. Secondly, we are expressing our love for our Father. Thirdly, we are offering ourselves totally to Him. We are giving ourselves back to the One who made us. And in this act of surrender, we are acceding to His Holy Will. It is a short ejaculation, but it says so much. It is, in essence, the most basic and direct form of consecration.

Q.   *Tell us about the Octaves in the Chaplet and the Consecration. Tell us about each of the themes. What do they mean?*

A.   The chaplet of *The Holy Octave of Consecration to God our Father* is made up of a Major Octave outlining Mankind's Salvation History and a Minor Octave detailing our approach to God our Father:

MAJOR OCTAVES

The Disobedience and Exile of God's Children

God Our Father was with us at the beginning in the Paradise He created for us—the Paradise of His Divine Will. Seduced by Satan, Adam and Eve chose not to do the Will of God and were, therefore, expelled from this Paradise and denied God's intimate presence. However, our Father promised that "the woman" would ultimately defeat the evil that had caused this separation—the evil of saying "No" to God's Will.

The Presence of God With His Children During Old Testament Times

Although God's children were expelled from Paradise by their choice not to do God's Will, God never abandoned them. He was present with them from the beginning. In Old Testament times, He manifested His presence through His own voice, the words of His Prophets, in the burning bush, in a pillar of smoke, and in the Ark of the Covenant. After God rescued His children from the bondage of Egypt, He requested that they celebrate the Feast of Tabernacles for eight days each year. He wanted them to remember that He loved them, He saved them, and He was present with them. Later when God was present in the Ark of the Covenant, Solomon built a magnificent Temple to house it. He then celebrated an eight-day Feast of Dedication in preparation for God's presence in the Temple. And God responded by manifesting His presence in a tangible and powerful way. At the close of the Old Testament, the Maccabees's re-instituted this eight-day feast to purify and re-dedicate the

Temple that had been defiled through pagan influence, so the Presence of God would dwell with them once more.

The Fiat of Mary Our Mother
Mary gave her "Yes" when the angel Gabriel came to her and asked her to be the mother of the Son of God. The Holy Spirit came upon her and the power of God our Father overshadowed her. In saying "Yes" to God's Will, Mary (the "woman") allowed God to be present with His children in a new way. She actually became the "New Ark," a living tabernacle of Jesus, the Second Person of the Holy Trinity—mankind's Savior—who with His Mother's cooperation, would restore the exiled children of God to their Father.

The Fiat of Jesus Our Savior
Jesus offered His "Yes" to God our Father during His Passion in the Garden of Gethsemani. Through His Passion, Death, and Resurrection, Jesus redeemed us, defeating the sin (saying "No" to God's Will) and death (separation and exile from God) which Satan introduced into the world. Through Jesus, His Church, and His Sacraments, we could now return to God our Father and have eternal life.

The Sending of the Holy Spirit
Before ascending to His Father, Jesus promised that He would not leave us as orphans. He asked God our Father to send the Holy Spirit. In doing this, God could again be present with us in a new way. It was now "possible" for God not only to be "with" us (as in Old Testament times), but "in" us.

The Choice of God's Children to Return to Their Father

As prodigal children of God our Father, we are given the opportunity (individually and collectively) to make a sincere, free-will decision to return to our Father's House. This means deciding to turn away from our own will, our own sinfulness, our own worldliness, and "convert" or turn back toward the presence of God our Father.

The Fiat of God's Children

In giving our "Yes" to God our Father, in agreeing to do His Will in all things, in giving ourselves completely to Him, He comes to dwell in us and we dwell in Him—we are home with our Father. We become temples of the Living God. In a sense, heaven and earth are joined: "Thy Kingdom come. Thy will be done on earth as it is in heaven."

The Coming of the New Jerusalem

The New Jerusalem is the eventual conclusion of our Salvation History—when heaven and earth will be transformed, when mankind will finally be fully restored to God our Father, and when God will manifest His presence and dwell with His children forever in a new way.

MINOR OCTAVE:

Praise: Praise God Our Father and His Creation.

Thanksgiving: Thank Him for all that He has done for you.

Offering: Offer Him all that He has given you.

Repentance: Ask for His forgiveness when you offend Him.

Inheritance: Acknowledge and celebrate that you

           are truly a child of God; embrace the
           joys and responsibilities.

Fiat: Say "Yes" to God's Will in all things.
Fidelity: Be loyal and persevering.
Consecration: Give yourself to God our Father.

Q   *How often should we pray the chaplet?*

A   I believe our Father gave us the chaplet as a means
of knowing, loving, and honoring Him. Our
Father wants us to have a loving, intimate relationship
with us. To have a loving, intimate relationship with
Him, we need to spend time with Him on a regular
basis. Ideally, we should pray the chaplet each day.
And, certainly, we should pray the formal chaplet
during the *Holy Octave of Consecration to God
our Father.*

CHAPTER ELEVEN

THE LOVE OF THE FATHER

Q. *Tell us about the love God the Father has for His people.*

A. How can I begin to explain how much our Father loves us? That has been the primary focus of all my dialogues with Him. And it is not an impersonal, intellectual love. It is a real love—very personal, intimate, and intense. His love for us is very protective, very tender, very involved, very vigilant. His loving Presence is with us always. He may at times "feel" far away, but this is how we "feel." It is our perception, not the truth and reality of God.

Q. *Tell us about the Father and each soul He creates.*

A. Because of His intense, passionate love for us, He desires that not one child be lost to Him. He wants every single one of us to come home. His love is illustrated in the parable of the shepherd who goes off to find the one lost sheep. Our Father wants us all.

It is difficult for us to realize that God made us, knows everything about us, has counted every hair on our heads, and knitted our very bones in our mother's womb. He knows us better than we know ourselves. We are His children, in the most real and total sense of the word.

He cares about everything that happens to us. He wants to be close to us. He wants to be part of our lives. He wants us to love Him as He loves us. Most importantly, He loves us in all times, in all places, in all situations—He loves us unconditionally.

Q. *Why do you think people are afraid of the Father?*

A. We are not born with fear or terror of our Creator, our Father. Instead, we learn to be afraid of Him. The word "fear" is used in Holy Scripture to describe how we should feel about our Father, but I do not believe the word is used in quite the same way we use it today. Most of us today think of fear as meaning that we are afraid of something that could hurt or kill us. I do not understand the use of the word in Scripture quite this way. I understand that the fear we should feel as God's children is twofold: (1) tremendous "awe" of our Father, (2) extreme apprehension over being separated from our Father. But we have somehow absorbed a mentality of fearing our own true Father. And this "fear" causes us to avoid Him.

This unfair and inaccurate picture of our Father has made if difficult, if not impossible, for His children to know and love Him—and it stands to reason that honoring someone we don't know or love would not be a priority for us. Because the true face of our Father has been hidden for so long, most of mankind has forgotten Him, put Him aside, or denied His very existence.

Q. *Why do most people only pray to Jesus? Has He*

spoken of this?

A.   I believe that if we could all climb to the top of a mountain and look down on mankind's salvation history, we would have a much better perspective of God's relationship with His children. We need to remember that our Father created us for His own Heart to be with Him forever, and that since man chose not to do God's Will and separate himself from eternal Life with God, our Father has grieved and been actively with us until we are one day restored to Him.

In this effort, our Father sent His Son Jesus to ransom us so we could return, to show us the way home, and to reveal the Truth that we are God's children. Jesus is also present with us and sustains us on our journey home to our Father. Jesus asked our Father to send the Holy Spirit to purify and refine us so that the Presence of God could dwell in us.

We must understand, then, that our Father sent Jesus and the Holy Spirit to us for the sole purpose of bringing us back home to Him. For some reason, however, we have confused the "way" with the end or goal of our journey. We misguidedly refuse to look beyond Jesus, forgetting that His mission was to shepherd and lead the prodigal children back home to their Father.

If we read the Gospels with a fresh perspective and highlight everything Jesus ever said, we would clearly see that He knows, loves, and honors His Father, and that He came to teach us to do the same. Jesus would be the first one to direct us to our Father. That is why our Father sent Him to us. We need only read the words of Jesus.

Yes, Jesus is also God and part of the Holy Trinity. But the Holy Trinity is relational. The Three Persons are not identical, nor are they one faceless entity. They are three distinct Persons. The mission of Jesus the Son and the Holy Spirit is to restore us to our Father. Because Jesus and the Holy Spirit are God, part of the Holy Trinity, we should also know, love, and honor Them. But we must not neglect our Father, nor should we forget that our only purpose for existing is to return to Him.

CHAPTER TWELVE

HONORING OUR FATHER

Q.   *Has the Father spoken to you about the fact that no churches are in His Name? That His honor is not very visible?*

A.   This is related to the previous question. We are a very Christ-centered Church, to the disadvantage of our Father and the Holy Spirit. I don't believe we can have a Trinitarian God and unequally focus on one member of that Trinity. We need to re-look at this as a relational process in the Holy Trinity. Jesus and the Holy Spirit moving us always toward our Father. We must remember that all things proceed from the Source, God our Father.

But because the Catholic Church focuses almost exclusively on Jesus, we see this reflected in the names of our churches, paintings, statues, prayers, hymns, devotions, etc.

God our Father wants us to honor Jesus, Mary, and the saints in this way. However, I believe He is saddened that we have forgotten Him—and surely we have. Ask yourself how we honor God our Father in the Church. This glaring oversight should serve as an unsettling epiphany.

Q.   *You said that the Father is desirous of consecration to Him using an 8-day (octave) consecration. Tell us about this consecration.*

A.   The most compelling precedent for consecrating ourselves to God our Father over an eight-day feast, or octave, is found in John 10:22-39. This passage describes how Jesus, during the eight-day Feast of Dedication, revealed that He was consecrated to God our Father. Jesus further explains that He consecrated Himself to our Father so we, too, could be consecrated in truth (Jn 17:19-21). The concept of "Consecration to God our Father" is crucial because, as Jesus tells us, "the hour is coming, and now is, when the true worshipers will worship the Father in spirit and truth, for such the Father seeks to worship him. God is a spirit, and those who worship him must worship in spirit and truth" (Jn 4:23-24). If we follow Jesus, if we model ourselves after Him, shouldn't we also consecrate ourselves to God our Father during an eight-day feast, so that we, too, can adore Him "in spirit and in truth?"

Q.   *Why 8 days? Is there some meaning to this? Is it Scriptural?*

A.   The concept of an "octave," or 8-day feast, has been significant in our relationship with God since the beginning of our salvation history. It is not by coincidence that Jesus chose to reveal His consecration to God our Father on the eight-day Feast of Dedication. Clearly, the octave symbolizes a designated period of time when God's children grow and God's relationship with them changes or is transformed.

Unlike other feasts and consecration methods, *The Holy Octave of Consecration to God our Father* views the "big picture" of our salvation history. It involves the entire process of our spiritual journey which includes Mary, our Mother; Jesus, our God and our Savior; and the Holy Spirit, our God and our Sanctifier—with progression always toward God our Father.

God's Word in both the Old and New Testaments provides us with extensive Scriptural support for an eight-day, or "octave," format. From the Book of Genesis to the Gospels and Epistles, the number "eight" is used to signify salvation, covenant, purification, and dedication. Perhaps, more importantly, it is used to indicate the end of one era and the beginning of another in which God is revealed, manifested, and present to His children in a new way.

Q. *What kind of feast day does the Father request?*

A. *The Holy Octave of Consecration to God our Father,* in its most powerful form, is intended as a formal eight-day feast for God our Father culminating on the first Sunday of the "eighth" month, God our Father's month—August. The solemn eighth day of *The Holy Octave of Consecration to God our Father* would be celebrated under the title of "The Feast of the Father of All Mankind." On this day, the children of God would come together to know, love, and honor their one true Father.

Q. *Is this related to Mother Eugenia Ravasio's (1932) revelations?*

A. Several years ago, I read the messages of Mother Eugenia and was stunned. I found them absorbing but also unsettling. I found them unsettling because I had never really thought of God our Father as a real person before—not one who really wanted to have a relationship with His children. And unsettling because I wasn't sure how to relate to more than one person in the Holy Trinity. It almost felt like I was being disloyal to Jesus, or worshiping more than one God. After I realized the relational process of the Holy Trinity and that we pass through the gate (Jesus) to get into the sheepfold (heart of our Father), I understood better. We are all intended for the heart of our Father. God our Father's message to Mother Eugenia helped me begin to think about these things and to discover my Father. Nearly a year later, I heard the voice of our Father tell me to look up—and that's when I saw the eight lights. That's when the work on *The Holy Octave of Consecration to God our Father* began.

Through both Mother Eugenia's messages and through the dialogue, our Father has asked for a feast—a feast entitled *The Feast of the Father of All Mankind*. He also asked that the feast be on the first Sunday of August, the eighth month.

For some reason, Mother Eugenia's messages were approved by the Church, but were sealed away without explanation. I believe *The Holy Octave of Consecration to God Our Father* is the fruition and culmination of that earlier effort.

Q. *Why is this Feast Day necessary? Why August?*

A.   I believe that our Father desires a special Feast that specifically honors Him. The Church has feast days for Jesus, the Holy Spirit, Mary, and the Saints—but none for our Father. Through the dialogue, I understand that this Feast Day is necessary at this time, that the Church is somehow incomplete until this is done. I also understand that this Feast is directly related to our Lady's Triumph and the Era of Peace.

This cannot be a feast for the sake of adding another feast to the Church calendar. Instead, it is what the Feast would accomplish: mankind understanding that God is our Father, that we choose to know, love, and honor Him, and that we say "Yes" to His will. This is accomplished by consecrating ourselves to Him and more clearly understanding the Holy Trinity.

I understand that our Lady will Triumph when the prodigal children return to their Father. Only then will the Era of Peace be granted because God will live among us in a new and special way. Our lives, our culture, will be built around God—God will not be separated and set apart from our daily lives.

Until we know, love, and honor our Father, how can the prodigal children return home? How can the children be reconciled with each other and with God? How can there be peace among men—the peace of God?

Our Father has asked for this Feast in August, specifically the first Sunday of August. This Consecration Feast, I believe, will help usher in a new era.

CHAPTER THIRTEEN

THE FATHER OF
ALL MANKIND

Q.   *Tell about the Eternal Father and His Fatherhood, as our Father?*

A.   When we read Holy Scripture, we see that our Father has always been with His prodigal children, from the day they exiled themselves from Him in Paradise to the present. He has never left us as orphans. His words and actions in Holy Scripture demonstrate that He is a loving, compassionate, protective father, not only in the Old Testament, but also as revealed by His Son Jesus in the New Testament. God's Fatherhood may seem distant and non-related to us, something in ancient books. "What does this have to do with us," we might ask. But it has everything to do with us—personally.

Jesus offered His life for each one of us, so that we might know the truth—that God is our true Father and we are His true children. These are not just words, it is reality. And God our Father desires a real relationship with each one of His children. He is the most tender of Fathers. Never absent, He is always with us—in every time, place, and circumstance.

He knows us intimately—He made us and has been present with us always He loves us completely, and wants us to choose to know, love, and honor Him so that we might live with Him eternally.

He cares for us like a tender mother with her babe and protects us like the fiercest warrior. He wants to be involved in every aspect of our lives.

God is "the" Father and His is "the" family—how great and wonderful and awesome this is—we are known, loved, cared for, and protected by the Creator of the entire universe, of all that is: He is our Father.

Q. *Why do you call him, "The Father of All Mankind."*

A. I refer to Him as the Father of All Mankind because that is what He refers to Himself as in the dialogue. This title is very important and illuminating because it establishes that (1) God is our Father and (2) He is the Father of all men—no exceptions. If we ponder this, we will realize that we are all brothers and sisters. We belong to one family and have one Father and one Mother. We are all made in the image and likeness of God, and God lives in all of us.

Certainly, if we truly understand the implications of this, we would never fight, never hate one another. We would freely choose to live in the peace and love of God.

When the world comes to embrace our Father and this title, peace will come to the world.

CHAPTER FOURTEEN

A PURIFICATION?

Q. *The Father speaks to you about teaching His children "after the storm." What does this means? What storm?*

A. Based on our Father's comments in the dialogue, I understand that an imminent upheaval is coming—in our Father's words, "Soon." I think this is supported by events that have been occurring during this century. As we evolve more and more into a Godless global culture, we generate consequences. I believe that the consequences for our ill-advised choices constitute the "storm," our Father refers to. We are bringing chaos and havoc down upon ourselves. As with storms in nature, there will be darkness and damage—but after this will be clearing and the fresh air of renewal and transformation.

After the storm our Father refers to is over, mankind will relate to Him differently. A transformation will have occurred, and life will be lived in a new way—life lived intimately with God our Father.

I understand that all the revelation and work that are taking place to help mankind see the true face of our Father are desperately needed.

Early in the dialogues, I symbolically saw a green valley with sheep—and Jesus, Mary, and the Apostles were up on the hillside watching over and caring for these sheep. There were passes at both ends of this valley. The sheep entered at one end through a narrow pass and exited at the other end—a very rocky, craggy pass. And as the sheep approached to pass through this opening, there was an intense, dark storm. A Cross of Light illuminated the sky above the opening. On the other side was a large, bleak, dry desert. And our Lady, Jesus, and the Apostles led the sheep. But there were sandstorms and many of the sheep wandered off. Finally, they came to a lush area near a great body of water. Here life was begun over again—simply and purely with God.

Q. *Has He spoken to you about chastisement? Have you had visions of the world in chastisement or after?*

A. Yes, I have had experiences during prayer where I have seen chastisement—again, I believe through man's own choices. During one experience, I was outside and across a great wide field of grain. I saw a city far off in the distance. Suddenly, the city exploded into smoke and flames; it was hot, red, and glowing. Another time, our Lady showed me the earth and it was desolate and there were men's bones scattered about. It seemed sterile and lifeless.

Not only did I see the vision of the valley, the storm, and the desert, as I mentioned previously, but I also saw a lush area near water which I believe represented a new way of life after the storm. I have also seen a radiant city where I was with our Father. However, the city was still empty. And our Father seemed to be waiting.

Q. *What is His plan for mankind, as you understand?*

A. God our Father's only plan for mankind is that His children return to Him—it is as simple as that. The more we pull away, run away, from our Father and His will, the farther we will have to go to return to Him, the more our hearts will be hardened, the more we will need to undergo to be purified and refined.

Our Father wants to live with us and in us forever—this is His plan for mankind.

Q. *Will many people die if there is a chastisement? Has He said?*

A. Again, our Father doesn't use graphic visions of death and destruction to terrify me. I see things symbolically and I understand what "could" be: desolate earth and bones, burning cities-or new life in God.

If only we understood what could happen if we keep making the wrong choices—choices not in God's will, but outside it. Desolation and death are the consequences of being outside God's will.

Q. *The Father speaks about all "being transformed into Him." What is this transformation?*

A. I understand that some sort of transformation will take place—man and the world will undergo a change. I don't quite know how to explain this except to say that God will be more fully in those

85

who invite Him, who are open to Him. This process will have an effect— those who are not prepared will experience great suffering, perhaps even death. But all will be reborn in God.

Q.   *Will all souls be transformed into Him?*

A.   This is God's sincere desire. This is God's will for His children. We can choose to be in or outside God's will. It is our choice.

Q.   *Has the Father spoken to you about suffering? About sin?*

A.   Suffering is a sacred thing. It brings us closer to God. When we suffer, we are like Jesus. When we suffer, we can choose to reach out to God, to ask Him to help us. This shows our dependence on God, our childlikeness. And we can choose to offer our suffering to God to be used for the good of our souls and the souls of others. No suffering should ever be wasted. It is a gift from God.

The term "sin" has fallen from favor in our times. However, all "sin" means is that we have chosen to do, say, or think something that is outside God's will. We have separated ourselves from God by our free will. God's will is where God is—it is Paradise, Heaven, His Kingdom—His heart.

CHAPTER FIFTEEN

THE COMING OF
THE KINGDOM

Q. *What is the most fascinating thing He has told you?*

A. That He loves Me and that I am His child–I belong to Him. This applies not only to me, but to all of us.

Q. *The Father has often spoken to you about David, Isaiah, Judith, Daniel, Abraham and other Old Testament figures. Have you seen these people in visions? Why are they so important now?*

A. I believe that our Father has used several figures and stories from the Old Testament to show me that they exist outside time and space to teach us in the present. They were not only relevant then, but for all times and places. There is a sense in the dialogues that something very profound is going to happen–soon. David, especially, has been an integral part of the dialogues. I have often seen David beckoning me, running ahead of me to the top of a hill where there was a newly built Church. But I haven't been allowed to go in. David shows it to me and smiles with great excitement and joy. Abraham was shown to me to teach me about fatherhood and sacrifice. Judith, Mary Magdalene, and Daniel demonstrated faith, fidelity, courage, and trust. Isaiah, Ezechial, Daniel,

Jeremiah, Hosea, Joel, and Micah revealed the prophetic element.

Q. *Has the Father spoken about Mary's apparitions?*

A. Yes, our Father has said that our Lady has come to mother us and prepare us to return to Him. He has specifically referred to Fatima and the Miracle of the Sun. Our Lady's mission will be completed when the one who attempts to separate us from God is defeated and we are restored to our Father.

Q. *Is now the time for the fulfillment of the Lord's prayer, "Thy Kingdom Come on Earth?"*

A. This has always been our Father's desire, His will. According to the prayer Jesus taught us, "Thy will be done. Thy Kingdom come on earth as it is in heaven." Doing God's will is necessary for the full coming of His Kingdom on earth. The process is on going and it comes in degrees, in stages. Where God is, there is His Kingdom. So the Kingdom is inside us, around us, and apart from us in a place we will go to after we die. As St. Paul tells us, we can only see through the glass darkly now. This will change, however, when Heaven touches earth. Through us, the Kingdom comes when we know, love, and honor our Father, when we give Him our fiat. It has been coming like small specks of light, connection points, but will come more fully when mankind embraces our Father. *The Holy Octave of Consecration to God our Father* will, I believe, help facilitate this. And our Father is asking for this now.

Q. *Are your messages in any way connected to*

Luisa Piccarreta's message about Divine Will and the Kingdom of the Divine Will on Earth?

A.   I am familiar with Piccarreta's writings in a general way, having read introductory material. I have not read her advanced works, however. My sense is that what she writes about may refer to what takes places after what is transpiring now. But again, I cannot respond to this question properly because I am not fully familiar with the material, nor has our Father spoke of it to me.

Q.   *How important is this Feast Day for the Father? What will it mean to the world? To the Church?*

A.   I think much has been leading up to this Consecration Feast Day. In a sense, the Church will be more "complete," having revealed and celebrated the Three Persons of the Holy Trinity more fully—especially the Source of All, God our Father. It will not be a "new" Church in the sense that it does away with the old. Rather, it is a more complete revelation and fulfillment of the Church—the prodigal children returning to their Father. Our Father's children will truly know, love, and honor Him—as well as the entire Holy Trinity. He will be with us, living with and in us in a new way. I understand that the Consecration Feast would bring the presence of God and His peace to the world in a way previously unknown to mankind.

Q.   *Is the Feast Day related to Mary's Triumph?*

A.   Yes, I believe it is. In the Book of Genesis, God tells us the woman (Mary) will crush his (Satan's) head. This passage is positioned between the disobedience of Adam and Eve (having been seduced by Satan) and the revelation of the consequences for this act (exile from our Father). My understanding is that Mary will triumph over Satan when the children of God are exiled no more, when they finally return back home to their Father. Jesus was sent to ransom us (pay for our sin) so we "could" return; He was also sent to show us the way back home. Jesus revealed the truth that God is our Father and we are His children, so that we could "choose" to have eternal life with our Father. He also sustains us and is present with us on that journey. Like Mary and Jesus, we, too, must freely offer our "Yes" to God's will. The Consecration Feast Day provides us with the opportunity to do all these things. When mankind *returns* to its Heavenly Father, Mary will have *triumphed* over the seducer who tempted the children into exile.

Q.   *Has He spoken about the Church and Mary's Final Dogma?*

A.   Yes, our Father says the Dogma is right and true. However, I have been asked to separate myself from the work of promoting the dogma. I was told by our Father that I would understand this later.

Q.   *Has the Father spoken about the Second Coming of Christ? Is this near?*

A.   Our Father has spoken only of His coming to us and the coming of His Kingdom.

Q.   *When does He want this Feast Day to be celebrated?*

A.   Our Father has asked that His Feast Day be celebrated on the first Sunday of August.

CHAPTER SIXTEEN

THE FEAST DAY, THE MEDAL, AND THE SCAPULAR

Q. *Tell us about the history and meaning of the medal?
    What does it signify with the harp on the back of the
    medal?*

A. In the dialogue our Father told me that He wanted a
    medal struck which should be given to each individual
    who consecrates himself to Him. He showed me what
    He desired for a medal, saying that the medal was His
    gift to us, that it showed His love for His children. He
    described it as a road map back home to Him. He
    asked that the medals be blessed, saying that many
    miracles would come about through the Consecra
    tion and Medal. Our Father explained that the medal
    should be worn as an outward sign to all His children
    and that embracing this symbol would show His
    children's love for Him.

    Therefore, a special medal was designed to illustrate the
    process of this consecration. On the front of the medal
    is the actual consecration process. God our Father is
    seen in Heaven reaching down to us on earth; man is
    seen on earth reaching up to God our Father in

Heaven. The force of God's love for us is shown in the rays that proceed down from His hand; the force of our love for Him is pictured in our "fiat" radiating up to Him. These rays intersect through the Cross of Jesus. This Cross is the bridge or link between God our Father and His children. At one end, it is grounded in the earth through Mary, our Mother. It then proceeds up through the sanctifying power of the Holy Spirit into Heaven at the other end. Eight lights, signifying the Scripturally-supported Octave, are shown on the horizontal beam of the Cross. These eight lights serve to guide us on our journey back home to God our Father.

The back of the medal displays the eight-stringed harp of David, as mentioned in Psalm 6. St. Augustine understood this mystically, as symbolizing the octave— seven days of this mortal life followed by the last resurrection and the world to come. And that during our mortal life, like David, we must also feel sorrow for our sins and repent of them while here on earth. On this eight-stringed harp we have placed the eight themes or steps of the Holy Octave of Consecration to God our Father—praise, thanksgiving, offering, repentance, inheritance, fiat, fidelity, and consecra-tion. Inside the bow of the harp are printed the words: "The rhythm and harmony of God's Will." This reminds us that when we pluck the eight strings or themes of this consecration to God our Father, a beautiful music ascends to heaven—we are choosing to live in the rhythm and harmony of His Will.

Q.   *The Father said He will come on August 1999. What does this mean?*

A. Our Father said He would come if mankind celebrated His Feast Day in 1999, which has been designated by the Church as the Year of our Creator and Father. My understanding is that our Father is telling us that if mankind knows, loves, and honors Him—if we love Him and give ourselves to Him—He will indeed come to be with and in us in a special spiritual way.

Q. *Tell us about the God the Father Scapular that He asked for. Why is it white?*

A. On day during dialogue, I saw laundered white, linen sheets hanging out to dry in the sun. My two grandmothers (who are deceased) and our Lady came out from behind the sheets. They had been tending them. Then our Father placed the white linen scapular in my opened hand and I was told that it signified our souls and that in offering ourselves to God, our souls must be clean and white. I was told that the scapular would serve as a visual aid, so that people would understand that in offering themselves to God, they must be cleansed and purified. The scapular looks the way our souls should look before God.

Q. *"Eight" is the Peace of God, the Father said. What does this mean?*

A. I understand the meaning of this on three levels: (1) "eight" signifies the end of one era and the beginning of a new one, e.g., the Sunday of a new week. (And for us in this time, the new era, I believe, will be an era of peace.), (2) the "eight" graphically illustrates two circles intersecting and flowing into each other—the higher into the lower and then the lower into the higher—God in us and us in God, the connection of

Heaven and earth, His Kingdom coming to earth as it is in Heaven, (3) the "eight" represents the Holy Octave which our Father referred to as an [eight-runged] ladder to Him. Through *The Holy Octave of Consecration*, we return to God and we are in His heart, His Kingdom, His will, His peace.

CHAPTER SEVENTEEN

FATIMA AND THE FATHER

Q. *Tell us about the Father and Fatima. Has He spoken of Himself being involved with the message of Fatima?*

A. Yes, our Father explained that Mary's Heart will Triumph when His children return to Him; that when this occurs, there will be an Era of Peace; and that the consequences of our choice was graphically depicted in the Miracle of the Sun at Fatima.

Q. *Tell us about the "Miracle of the Sun" at Fatima with the Father. What about Russia?*

A. In the dialogue, our Father explained that He was represented in the sun at Fatima's Miracle of the Sun. He showed me that when the sun danced in the sky and its many colors seemed to penetrate everything it touched, that He was trying to show us that He is with and in us— in all His creation. He also showed me that when the sun fell toward earth, this was an attempt to show us that He was coming to us.

The reaction of many was sheer terror. The people weren't ready. And He also wanted me to know that we have choices and that there are consequences for our choices. I was made to understand that the power of the sun was used specifically to demonstrate that if we continued to pursue and apply knowledge (Science, Medicine, Technology, etc.) "outside" His will, that we would reap the consequences (possibly nuclear consequences which "ape" the power of the sun). However, if we chose God and His will, our Father would come and warm us (as He did to the cold and rain-soaked people at Fatima) and fill us up with His love and peace.

The choice is ours. That's what my understanding is of the Miracle of the Sun at Fatima.

Q. *The Father said to you, "All that is present will cease and become new." What does this mean? When will it happen?*

A. Our Father is referring to transformation here. Only our Father knows the time when this will be accomplished. Again, my understanding is that all will be made new "in" God. God is present in His creation now, but He will be present more fully and in a new and different way. As the world pulls farther and farther away from God, the time for consequences and eventual transformation comes ever closer. Our Father has often said, "Soon."

Q. *Who are the Remnant that the Father speaks of to you?*

A. When our Father uses the term "Remnant" I believe He is referring to those who are in union with Him, in the rhythmand harmony of His will. Those who have been loyal. Those who know love, and honor God—

the entire Holy Trinity, all Three Persons. Those who have overcome all obstacles to the Father.

Remnant indicates a part that remains after the remainder of the whole is removed. Many of God's children have been absorbed into our worldly culture, leaving a "remnant" that has stayed loyal to God—those who have and will survive these times of purification. Remnant can also pertain to those who are left after a chastisement. However, this term should never be used in an *elitist* sense. We must always remember that it is God's will that not one of His little ones be lost.

Q. *Should people store food and prepare?*

A. I think it is good to want to live a more simple, basic life— closer to God and His creation. But I have not been given any indication in the dialogue that we should head for the hills and store food and water. I'm not certain if this is necessary or appropriate for the consequences we may be enduring. I think the most important thing is to know, love, and honor God our Father—and trust in Him always.

Q. *What do you know about the "purifying fire" that He told you about? He told you it "will sweep across the planet." Is this a real fire? A nuclear fire? A spiritual fire?*

A. Only God knows in what form this purifying fire will come. I know only its purpose—it will purify us. This may be strictly spiritual, or it may be physical. Perhaps it will be both. Whatever its form, it will serve to purify us. This is not necessarily bad or frightening—

mankind and the entire planet are in great need of cleansing and purification.

Q. *What does this mean when He says, "The end of an era is hurtling toward you, My children."*

A. Based on the dialogues, I believe that we are moving swiftly toward the end of one era and the beginning of the next. In this particular phrase, I believe our Father meant that the end of this era is fast approaching because of our own choices and decisions. We are causing a set of circumstances to occur in this world that will most definitely have destructive consequences—physically and spiritually. We have only to look at the world today and see that this is true.

Q. *You had visions of a powerful man rising. The Father said, "This man means to break the back of My children." Who is this man? Is he the antichrist?*

A. Several times in the dialogue and readings there have been references to a powerful man rising. In prayer, I have seen a man at what appeared to be a rally. There seemed to be economic and political chaos. This man assured the people that everything would be all right. That the world could be united. That we could be better than we had ever been. But this was an empty promise because he was offering a "Godless" peace—this was not the peace of God. Unfortunately, no one at the rally seemed to notice or care about this omission.

I have also been given readings from Daniel regarding the anti-christ. These readings specifically refer to a person who would disregard God's Laws, making his own. Our Father seems to be emphasizing the importance of "His Laws" in this time.

Q.   *What is the meaning behind the messages that speak of a "new Heaven and a new earth?" The new Jerusalem? Is this the same as the writings in the Book of Revelation? The same as given to Father Gobbi?*

A.   Mankind has been moving toward the New Jerusalem —a new Heaven and a new earth, the City of God— since the beginning of mankind's salvation history when we lost Paradise. God has promised us this in Scripture, especially in the Book of Revelation.

I understand the New Jerusalem to be that point in time when mankind will be "fully" reunited with its Father—when God will be present with and in His children in a new way. Again, some sort of transformative purifying process will need to take place for this to happen.

I assume that the "New Jerusalem" referred to in the dialogue and Father Gobbi's messages are the same. However, I cannot authoritatively comment on this because I have not closely studied Father Gobbi's messages, nor has our Father spoken to me about them.

CHAPTER EIGHTEEN

GETTING CLOSER TO OUR FATHER

Q. *What does the Father mean when He speaks of the Rhythm and Harmony of His will?*

A. Our Father's will is like beautiful music. When we are in our Father's will, we are in "sync" with Him; we are immersed in the rhythm and order of it; we are in complimentary harmony. When we are outside our Father's will, we are not in sync with Him; we are outside the rhythm and order of it; and our lives are discordant.

When instruments and voices are out of tune, out of rhythm, and out of harmony, the music is unpleasant because it is discordant. This is what we are like when we are outside God's will.

Q. *How can we get closer to the Father's will?*

A. Our relationship with our Father begins by spending time with Him. This can be done through the Sacraments or by praying the Chaplet and other prayers. It can also be done without praying or talking, by quieting ourselves and becoming immersed in His presence. We can share our joys and sorrows with Him. We can also ask Him for His help. Or we can request that He guide us in our daily lives. And always, we can come to Him when we have offended Him and ask for His mercy and forgiveness.

Our Father desires to have an intimate relationship with us all. As we begin to know, love, and honor Him, we become more and more immersed in His Holy will. Gradually, we begin to more closely resemble our Father in thought, word, and deed.

When we are uncertain about God's will in any given situation, we can ask ourselves what our Father would want us to do. We can refer back to His Commandments and Jesus' teaching. Every time we say, "I love you, Father, and I give myself to you," we are freely offering ourselves to Him and asking Him to take us to Himself. And where our Father is, that is Paradise, Heaven, His Kingdom—His holy will.

Q. *Can we come to hear His voice, too? He has said hearing His voice "is possible for all of you," hasn't He?*

A. Yes, I believe all of us are born with the right equipment – our soul. As temples of the Holy Spirit, I believe all children of God are capable of hearing the voice of their true Father.

We hear the voice of God in Holy Scripture, in each other, and deep within our hearts. The children of God have been in exile since our first parents left Paradise, so our Father may seem very far away. But He has never abandoned us. He is always with us.

If we slow down our pace, if we take time to spend with our Father, if we quiet ourselves and listen—we will hear His voice inside us.

This is not to say discernment isn't needed. But a complicated set of instructions isn't needed for the children of God to speak to their Father and to listen to His voice. This is a gift we are all born with—it is part of our inheritance as the children of God.

Q.   *The Father speaks of a new ark? Can you explain?*

A.   To understand how our Father is using the term "ark" now, it would help to view it from a historical perspective: (1), Noah's ark housing and physically saving "eight" people in a worldwide purification; (2) the Ark of the Covenant housing the presence of God; (3) Mary becoming the "new ark," housing the presence of God (Jesus); and (4) the children of God becoming the ark, when through the Holy Spirit, the presence of God dwells in them, as in a tabernacle. In all these cases, the evolution of the "ark" has involved movement into a new era.

What is the "ark" in these times? Our Father says that when we are contained and consumed in His love, nothing can harm us. He refers to this as the ark of His love. He also says that when we have found our way back home—back to His heart, His love—that we are safe. He is in our heart and we are in His. In the dialogue our Father explains that the consecration must go on this ark. My understanding of this is that when the presence of God dwells in us, we also dwell in the presence of God. When we have found our way to the heart of our Father, we are finally home. We are safe and protected. And to find our home to His heart, he has given us *The Holy Octave of Consecration.*

CHAPTER NINETEEN

SEEING WITH THE EYES OF OUR SOUL

Q.   *How do we learn to "See with the eyes of our soul?"*

A.   God has given us the senses of sight, sound, taste, touch, and smell, so that we can perceive our physical world. However, through my experience with our Father, I have come to understand that we are entering a period of time when God is going to be present with and in us in a fuller way. St. Paul said we now see through a glass darkly. But I believe, as the coming of God's Kingdom approaches, as Heaven more fully intersects with earth, we will be better able to apprehend God's presence within our "souls." We will be more sensitive and responsive to God's presence.

I cannot explain it better than to say it is like a spiritual evolutionary process. We've always had the ability, I think. We are born with the ability. However, at this point in mankind's salvation history, we will begin to explore, discover, and improve our ability to apprehend God through our souls while we are yet in our physical bodies.

Does this mean that we will eventually see God with our physical eyes? I only know that for now He is asking us to know, love, and honor Him better by seeing Him with the eyes of our soul. It is as if Heaven and earth are intersecting within us.

When I see our Father with the eyes of my soul, something inside me resonates, like a chord is being struck within me that vibrates on a spiritual frequency allowing me to apprehend our Father in a way my human eyes cannot.

How do we see our Father with the eyes of our soul? This faculty is developed by spending quiet time with our Father: praying, speaking to our Father about our daily joys and sorrows, asking Him to help and guide us. And then by sitting in silence, basking in the warmth of His presence, listening to His gentle voice inside us. As we develop our relationship with our Father, as we come to know, love, and honor Him more, we will begin to apprehend His presence with and in us more fully. We will come to know Him as a "real" person. We will have found our Father.

Q.   *What does the Father mean when He says, "Teach My children that they must rely entirely on Me?"*

A.   Most of us think we are self-sufficient or that we need the help of other human beings to function and survive. But not many people will admit that they need God. Today, mankind thinks it has an answer and solution for everything. How foolish this must seem to our Father. What I have learned through the dialogue is that if we are going to survive, individually and collectively, we must rediscover and embrace our intimate relationship with God—He is our Father and we are His children. And as children we must look to our Father for all things, great and small, in our lives. Certainly, this doesn't mean we sit passively, expecting our Father to give us everything we "want." Rather, it means that we can, in trust, depend on our Father to provide us with our daily bread—for those things we need to survive physically and thrive spiritually. When we cooperate with our Father's will, He helps us help ourselves and each other.

What our Father is trying to teach us is to relate to Him as trusting children who look to their Father for sustenance, help, guidance—but most of all, love. This means letting go and letting God. In its most perfect form, this is "living in the will of our Father."

Q.   *Tell us what the Father has said to you about the gift of "choices" and about "consequences."*

A.   God has given each one of us the opportunity to choose. This is a gift of freedom. We have the perfect freedom to choose or not to choose God and His holy will. God has given each one of us the gift of free-will choice. This is how much He values us. He did not create us as puppets or slaves. Instead, He made us so that we had the perfect freedom to choose. There is no coercion or oppression in our relationship with our Father. There is only love.

There are consequences for our choices—a built-in cause/effect factor. When we choose God and His holy will, the consequence is eternal life in God. When we make choices that are opposed to God and His holy will, the consequence is separation from God because we place ourselves outside His will.

This concept of consequences is important because it helps us understand that God does not separate Himself from us; we separate ourselves from Him. It also helps us see that our bad choices set up a causal chain reaction that produces effects that hurt, damage, and destroy us and those around us, sometimes for generations. Ultimately, it is not God that will destroy us if we continue to make bad choices. It will be ourselves.

CHAPTER TWENTY

SPREADING DEVOTION
TO OUR FATHER

Q. *What did the Father mean when He told you to "build the Church and I will come?"*

A. I believe our Father meant this on three levels: (1) the Church in general, (2) actual physical churches, and (3) our hearts—the temples of His indwelling Presence. I believe when we, as a "Church," know, love, and honor our Father, He will come to us in a new and special way. I also think that our Father is asking us to glorify Him by building churches or chapels in His honor. And always, our Father is requesting that we build the church, tabernacle, or temple, that is our heart, so that His presence may dwell in us.

Q. *Should people spread the new devotion more?*

A. Yes, our Father wants to draw all His children to Himself in this time. It is by means of this devotion that we will come to know, love, and honor Him more fully. Again, I believe that the return of the children of God to their Father is directly related to our Lady's Triumph and the Era of Peace. Therefore, the spread of this devotion is timely.

Q.   *Is the Father still speaking to you?*

A.   Yes, during dialogues. It is my understanding that our Father wants to have an intimate relationship with all of us.

Q.   *How has your family responded to all of this?*

A.   Some family members have been very supportive of the work.

Q.   *Has the Church investigated your experiences?*

A.   Yes, the Church has begun to investigate my experiences.

Q.   *Do you have a spiritual director? Have any theologians studied these revelations?*

A.   Yes, a Catholic priest with a background in spiritual direction and Canon Law is serving as my spiritual director and another priest, an experienced and well-respected theologian, is acting as an advisor.

Q.   *Do you publicly speak of these messages and experiences?*

A.   I speak privately about our Father to my family and publicly through my writing. But as a wife, mother, and grandmother, I do not feel called to leave my family to speak publically. I believe the written work serves that purpose.

Q.   *How has your life in the Father changed you?*

A.   My life has changed dramatically. Before I was very much engaged with the culture. Now, I focus on our Father and my family. Our Father is the central core of my life. Everything flows from that relationship. Not only do I better recognize the presence of our Father with us, but also in us. This has given me a profound appreciation and love for all other human beings.

Q.   *Tell us about your love for the Father of All Mankind.*

A.   I have come to know only one true thing—and that is my love for our Father and the Father's love for me and for all His children. When you love our Father, He is in your thoughts always—even when you are actively engaged with something else. You see Him in His creation, in other people. You come to depend on Him for comfort and guidance. You are constantly in awe of His creation and, most of all, the realization that He is your true Father and you are His true child. You want to please Him by doing His will in all you think, say, and do. And when you do something that offends Him or another person, you feel genuine sorrow.

I also realize that our Father is a real person, and this is who you fall in love with—not an abstract, intellectual concept. This intimate relationship becomes the most important thing in your life. He is all good, all merciful, all loving. He is gentle and yet powerful. He is kind; He has a sense of humor; He loves us beyond all human reason. He loves us unconditionally. How could I not love our Father? He is love.

Q.   *How should souls approach the Father?*

A.   I would suggest that we approach our Father with

awe, humility, an open heart, trust, and confidence. We can do this through the Sacraments and through our quiet time with Him. We should always seek Him out and invite Him into our lives, because He is always there for us. We should especially approach Him in a quiet environment, with an attitude of giving, not taking. We should praise and adore Him. And rely on Him for all we need.

Most importantly, we mustn't be "afraid" of Him. We should respect Him above all things and we should feel fear of ever offending Him or being separated from Him. But never should we be afraid of Him. This type of fear separates us from Him and keeps us from approaching Him. He is our all merciful and loving Father and we are His prodigal children. He loves us unconditionally—despite of and because of our weaknesses.

In approaching our Father, in establishing a personal, intimate relationship with Him, we learn how to better resemble the Father who made us in His own image.

Q.   *How should the world approach the Father?*

A.   The world can approach our Father in the same way. He, first and foremost, wants us to embrace Him as our true Father and to recognize that we are His true children. Second, He has given us *The Holy Octave of Consecration* so that all His children can individually and collectively know, love, and honor Him. This Consecration Feast Day, then, serves both to regather all His children and to restore them to their one true Father.

Through this, I believe that our Father will be with us in a special way. His Era of Peace will be granted to the world, and His Kingdom will come on earth as it is in heaven more fully.

When we know our Father, we will know "His Peace."

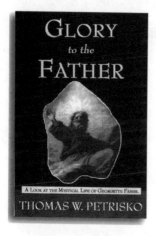

115

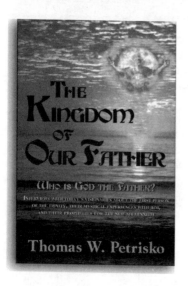
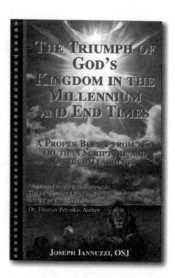

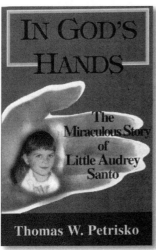
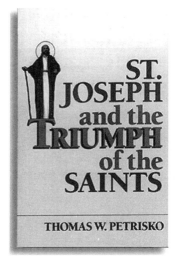

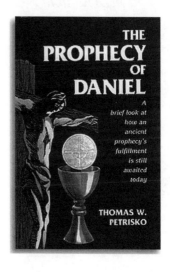
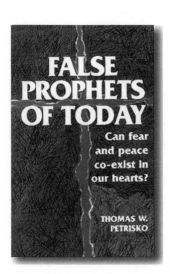

118

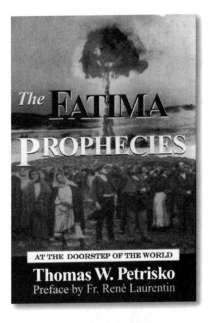

119

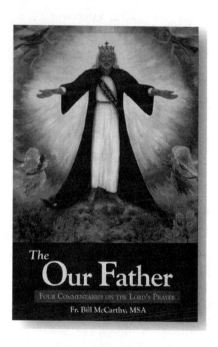